Disruptive Technologies in International Business

Disruptive Technologies in International Business

Challenges and Opportunities for Emerging Markets

Edited by
Alka Maurya, J. Mark Munoz, Loveleen Gaur
and Gurinder Singh

DE GRUYTER

ISBN 978-3-11-073859-9
e-ISBN (PDF) 978-3-11-073413-3
e-ISBN (EPUB) 978-3-11-073422-5

Library of Congress Control Number: 2023932399

Bibliographic information published by the Deutsche Nationalbibliothek
The Deutsche Nationalbibliothek lists this publication in the Deutsche Nationalbibliografie;
detailed bibliographic data are available on the internet at http://dnb.dnb.de.

Advance Praise for *Disruptive Technologies in International Business*

"Say the words distributive technologies and what comes to mind are Silicon Valley, DC, New York, and London. But far away from the tech zones of the developed countries, a revolution is brewing in developing countries. From Haiti to India, innovative and disruptive technologies are changing the face of international business. Maurya, Munoz, Gaur and Singh, along with a powerful group of experts, have tackled the important issue of cross pollination of knowledge and innovation – but this time with an eye on the emergence of disruptive technologies from the Global South. A timely and powerful book."

–Dr. Al Naqvi, CEO, American Institute of Artificial Intelligence

"*Disruptive Technologies in International Business* is a great introduction to the underlying technologies that are changing international business and, as a result, our daily lives as well. The authors and contributors cover a plethora of use cases, from marketing and smart cities to daily surface mobility, where many of us have already felt the impact of disruption in our daily lives. The book is insightful, with contributions from an impressive array of subject matter experts. I would highly recommend it for students, practitioners and anyone else who seeks insight and understanding of technology implications to their strategic business plans."

–Mike Srdanovic, Emerging Technology and Data Science
Practice Lead – Northern Trust

"This edited book titled *Disruptive Technologies in International Business* is an excellent anthology and a potpourri of various chapters that address many significant aspects of Disruptive Technologies (DT) in various parts of the world, such as India, Japan and some island economies. These DTs, i.e. Cloud, 5G, additive manufacturing, AI, IoT and Blockchain, are changing the way international business is being conducted and this book is enlightening us in the most efficient and effective scientific and empirical manner with excellent examples from all over the world."

–Marios I. Katsioloudes, PhD, Professor of Strategy and Entrepreneurship and
Dean, Faculty of Business Administration and Economics, American
University of Cyprus and Special Scientist with the University of Cyprus

https://doi.org/10.1515/9783110734133-202

Contents

Alka Maurya and J. Mark Munoz

Chapter 1
Introduction: Disruptive Technologies and their Implications for International Business

In recent years technology has completely changed the way organizations function. Disruptive technologies like artificial intelligence (AI), Internet of Things (IoT), cloud, 5G, additive manufacturing, and blockchain are revolutionizing the economics of trade and global production, empowering businesses of all sizes to make, move, and market products and services worldwide and with greater ease than ever before (Suominen, 2019).

AI, a computer's ability to process data and produce results in a way that is comparable to how humans learn, make decisions, and solve problems, is being used extensively in almost all managing business operations like e-commerce, marketing, transportation, manufacturing, and human resource management, to name a few. According to a study by PwC by 2030 AI could contribute around $15.7 trillion to the global economy, out of which $6.6 trillion is likely to come from increased productivity and $9.1 trillion from consumption-side effects (PwC, 2017). AI will act as a catalyst in promoting international business as it has immense potential to contribute to areas such as development and management of global value chains, trade using digital platforms, trade negotiations, etc. (Brookings, 2018).

IoT, another technology that has disrupted business, is ingrained in our daily lives through applications like intelligent transportation tracking, industrial wireless automation, public safety, personal health monitoring, health care for the elderly, etc. Many countries are working on making smart cities, which has resulted in a steep increase in demand for this technology. According to a study by McKinsey, the number of businesses that use IoT technologies has increased from 13% in 2014 to about 25% in 2018, and it is assumed that the worldwide number of IoT-connected devices is projected to increase to 43 billion by 2023, an almost threefold increase from 2018 (McKinsey & Company, 2019). This technology is finding a way into our day-to-day life and the potential of this technology appears to be limitless.

Additive manufacturing, also known as 3D printing, is disrupting manufacturing processes. This unique manufacturing technique supports the creation of three-dimensional solid items with a computer and printer. An object is built in an additive technique by laying down successive layers of material until the object is complete. 3D printing was invented in 1980s, but it has not yet made noticeable inroads in manufacturing. In 2018, revenues from 3D printing were less than 0.1% of global manufacturing revenue. Global revenue from 3D printing was $9.8 billion in 2018, as

https://doi.org/10.1515/9783110734133-001

compared to global manufacturing revenues of $12.8 trillion. It is expected that by 2023 share of additive manufacturing will be around 1% of global manufacturing revenue (World Economic Forum, 2020). It is predicted that due to 3D printing global trade will decline whereas global investment and trade in raw materials will increase (Freund, Mulabdic, & Ruta, 2020).

Further, Blockchain technology is seen as a revolution in terms of its potential to revolutionize supply chain management by facilitating traceability of traded goods, international payment wherein a letter of credit can be issued in as little time as four hours, record keeping and transparency in information sharing, digitalization of the entire rules of origin process at every stage, addressing the challenges of cross-border data exchanges between public agencies or authorities and private companies. modernize Single Windows for Foreign Trade (VUCEs) to name a few (Barafani, Garcia, & Rozemberg, 2021).

Though these technologies are extensively being used in developed countries, emerging economies are also not far behind either. This book is an attempt to understand how these technologies and their applications will contribute to the advancement of international business.

This book is organized and contextualized in such a way that the reader gains some technological understanding alongside its business applicability across borders. The featured chapters offer a collage of insights on how these technologies can potentially change the playing field in businesses and countries and contribute to the betterment of society.

Following this introductory chapter, the book is organized as follows:

Chapter 2, "Disruptive Technologies and Global Value Chain: Insights from SMEs in Emerging Markets" (Virginia Hernández, Antonio Revilla, and Alicia Rodríguez), provides insights on how data-related technologies are associated with the firm's propensity to be part of a global value chain (GVC).

Disruptive technologies are used not only by companies for improved decision-making but by policy makers as well. Chapter 3, "Digital Democratization: The Case of Environmental Risk Management in Haiti" (Nathalie de Marcellis-Warin, J. Mark Munoz, Hugo Warin, and Thierry Warin), provides insights on how drones are used as a decision-making tool for framing public policies. How drones can collect geographical data, in all dimensions of the term geography: natural, ecological, human activity, etc., in areas at high risk of natural disasters and how this data can help in better decision-making.

Internet-enabled devices have found their way into the modern vacation to reduce friction for the guest while gathering valuable data that can be used for creating targeted marketing campaigns and improving operational efficiencies. Chapter 4, "IoT in Tourism" (Richard "RJ" Podeschi II), explores the use of RFID technology to improve the guest experience and achieve operational efficiencies at the famed Orlando resort, and how Disney has paved the way for other popular tourist destinations around the world.

Chapter 5, "Internet of Things and Smart Cities as Accelerators for International Business," focuses on how the use of IoT, allows an ongoing exchange of information, knowledge, and innovation, generating economies of scope, reducing transportation and logistics costs, and improving interaction with customers and other stakeholders based on immediate and broad feedback. IoT helps to satisfy the growing global population's needs without compromising the environment, which is crucial given the threats that Anthropocene inevitably brings. IoT and Smart Cities can be a feasible solutions to cope with the environmental problems currently faced by mankind.

There are implications of IoT for project management within international business. Implications mainly include the handling and consumption of large amounts of data produced during the Project Management Life Cycle (PMLC) and how the data should be used in a constructive manner toward successful project execution. Chapter 6, "The Internet of Things (IoT) in Project Management" (Letitia Larry), analyses some aspects of the use of IoT in project management.

The application of disruptive technologies in Surface Mobility is the theme of Chapter 7 of this book. This chapter titled "The Rise of Surface Mobility in India" (Soma Arora) is an ode to the surface mobility business, which has risen, in the last two decades and is focused on the value proposition of this novel business model, where GoCar is the aggregator for GoMMT, a company servicing ticketing and accommodation needs for travelers, GoCar services the needs for road travelers in their landing destinations and other transitions within cities.

Chapter 8, "Digital Marketing and Globalization: The Opportunity for Caribbean Small Island Developing States" (Guido Rojer Jr.), elaborates on how digital marketing helps in taking the business to a global level. With reference to Caribbean Small Island Developing States (SIDS) the chapter provides insights on how these SIDS have embraced digital transformation to access the global market

The impact of technology is also visible in anime, which is hand-drawn and computerized animation. Chapter 9, a case study on "Japanese Anime: Redefining Digital Storytelling" (Aditya Kumar Gupta, Ashutosh Pillai, and Neelash Thallam), analyzes Japanese anime's journey and its growth in the digital space. This interesting case also focuses on the role of technology in the growth and revival of this amazing art of storytelling.

IoT has open plethora of opportunities for data collection, however, the security of personal data gathered in the process cannot be guaranteed. New vulnerabilities are constantly being discovered, "Crossing All Borders – The Future of IoT" (Ron Sheffield), Chapter 10 provides answers to questions such as, is IoT good? What is the future of IoT? Where are the boundaries between productivity and private independence?

Each of these chapters advances the understanding of technological applications in business within an international paradigm. the insights provided will be valuable to academics as they seek to learn more about the business and technology nexus. Business practitioners will find the innovative approaches inspiring and can potentially find new pathways toward business or product development; government officials, international organizations, and policy makers can find new leads toward more efficient systems, policies, and operational frameworks in our growingly technology-driven society.

Each of the featured technologies offer many advantages but there are accompanying risks, challenges, and disadvantages as well (Kavanagh, 2019). Many organizations have directed their efforts toward the application of these technologies to advance a specific organizational agenda, but the need of the hour is to also address concerns on the impact of these technologies on the environment, society, and economy. We hope that this book will contribute in a small way toward technological and business pursuits that address the needs of our global business community.

References

Barafani, M., Garcia, P. M., & Rozemberg, R. (2021, July 29). *Blockchain Technology: A New Opportunity for International Trade*. Retrieved January 25, 2022, from Inter-American Development Bank: https://blogs.iadb.org/integration-trade/en/blockchain-technology-a-new-opportunity-for-international-trade/

Brookings. (2018, December 13). *The Impact of Artificial Intelligence on International Trade*. Retrieved December 14, 2021, from https://www.brookings.edu/research/the-impact-of-artificial-intelligence-on-international-trade/

Freund, C., Mulabdic, A., & Ruta, M. (2020, September). *Is 3D Printing a Threat to Global Trade? The Trade Effects You Didn't Hear Abou*. Retrieved January 15, 2022, from World Bank.

Kavanagh, C. (2019, August 28). *New Tech, New Threats, and New Governance Challenges: An Opportunity to Craft Smarter Responses?* Retrieved March 10, 2022, from Carnegie Endowment for International Peace: https://carnegieendowment.org/2019/08/28/new-tech-new-threats-and-new-governance-challenges-opportunity-to-craft-smarter-responses-pub-79736

McKinsey & Company. (2019, July 22). *Growing Opportunities in the Internet of Things*. Retrieved March 25, 2022, from McKinsey & Company: https://www.mckinsey.com/industries/private-equity-and-principal-investors/our-insights/growing-opportunities-in-the-internet-of-things

PwC. (2017). *Sizing the Prize: PwC's Global Artificial Intelligence Study: Exploiting the AI Revolution*. Retrieved January 20th, 2022, from PwC Global: https://www.pwc.com/gx/en/issues/data-and-analytics/publications/artificial-intelligence-study.html

Suominen, K. (2019). *Revolutionizing World Trade: How Disruptive Technologies Open Opportunities for All*. Stanford: Stanford University Press.

World Economic Forum. (2020, January). *3D Printing: A Guide for Decision-Makers January 2020 In Collaboration with Mitsubishi Chemical Holdings Corporation*. Retrieved March 25, 2022, from World Economic Forum: https://www3.weforum.org/docs/WEF_Impacts_3D_Printing_on_Trade_Supply_Chains_Toolkit.pdf

Virginia Hernández, Antonio Revilla, and Alicia Rodríguez

Chapter 2
Disruptive Data-Related Technologies and Global Value Chain: Insights from SMEs in Emerging Markets

Introduction

The emergence of novel digital technologies is disrupting the configuration of global value chains (GVCs) in most industries, which is creating new opportunities for entrepreneurial businesses that can access rapidly changing GVCs (Fernández & Rodríguez, 2023). In particular, small and medium-sized enterprises (SMEs) from emerging markets (hereinafter, SME-EMs), which tend to face resource and capability constraints as a result of their smaller size and unfavorable institutional context, can derive significant advantages from their participation in GVCs. The engagement in international operations exposes them to developed institutional settings (Wu & Deng, 2020), innovative technological knowledge, a variety of cultures and markets, and advanced business practices by the chain's lead firms. This may lead to upgrades in the firm's capabilities (Humphrey & Schmitz, 2002), turning participation in GVCs into a source of competitive advantage.

SME-EMs, however, may experience significant competitive challenges in gaining access to GVCs, not least because of the informational barriers linked to limitations in accessing and processing information across borders (Hosseini et al., 2019). In this chapter, we address the question of how digital data technologies may help SME-EMs overcome such barriers and gain access to GVCs. In doing so, we contribute to the emerging research stream analyzing the relationships between digital technologies and global value chains (Brun, Gereffi, & Zhan, 2019; Fernández & Rodríguez, 2023; Opazo-Basáez et al., 2022; Strange & Zucchella, 2017). More concretely, we advance previous studies connecting digital technologies with the likelihood to participate in GVCs (Kos & Kloppenburg, 2019), in three ways. Firstly, we untangle the effects of different technologies depending on their role in the process of managing data and information: data gathering and storage (smart devices and cloud computing), data analysis and sensemaking (big data and artificial intelligence), and data sharing and monitoring (blockchain). Secondly, we extend the arguments and findings from previous research to the specific case of SME-EMs.

Acknowledgements: This research is part of projects TED2021-130042B-I00, funded by MCIN/AEI/ 10.13039/501100011033 and by the European Union NextGenerationEU/ PRTR; and PID2019-106874GB-I00/ AEI/10.13039/501100011033, funded by the Government Research Agency of Spanish Ministry of Science and Innovation.

https://doi.org/10.1515/9783110734133-002

Thirdly, we do not treat SMEs as a homogeneous category, but distinguish between micro-enterprises, small, and medium businesses, further exploring the firm size modulates the effects of the adoption of data-related technologies.

We build up the chapter as follows. First, we provide a brief theoretical overview on the different data-related technologies and their impact on the participation in GVCs by SME-EMs. Next, we describe the sample, variables, and methodology used in this study, followed by the main empirical findings, and a discussion and conclusion section.

Theoretical Background

Digital Technologies and Insertion into GVCs: Upgrading Opportunities for SME-EMs

The concept of GVC refers to the way several firms are interconnected across national borders, developing a full range of activities carried out on a global scale within a value-added production process (Gereffi & Fernandez-Stark, 2011; Hernández & Pedersen, 2017). Technology can play a crucial role ensuring coordination and cooperation among the different players involved in GVCs. Digital technologies have the potential to enhance information and knowledge sharing across geographies, improve connectivity, help build mutual trust (Dilyard et al., 2021), and facilitate buyers-supplier relationships (Veile et al., 2021). Unsurprisingly, digital technologies are reshaping the way GVCs are configured and managed (Fernández & Rodríguez, 2023; Wang & Hsu, 2021) and improving the outcomes of firms that take part in them (Opazo-Basáez et al., 2022). This brings up distinct opportunities for SME-EMs, which have been traditionally seen to adopt subsidiary roles in GVCs as dependent suppliers of lead firms. Digitalization may allow these firms to upgrade their positions in the value chain (Oliveira et al., 2021), take more active roles, build up their capabilities, and ultimately improve their competitiveness.

Disruptive Data-Related Technologies: Gathering, Analysis, and Sharing Technologies

Previous literature has included a range of emerging data-related technologies in the umbrella concept of Industry 4.0 (Dilyard et al., 2021; Opazo-Basáez et al., 2021). This includes cloud computing, smart devices, augmented reality, AI, blockchain, and big data analytics, among others. Although the business implications of these technologies vary, they have, taken together, the potential to disrupt the way value chains are configured and managed.

Digital technologies create integrated ecosystems in which information flows in all directions, analytics enable adjustment, and response takes place in real time throughout the value chain (PWC, 2016; Ferrantino & Koten, 2019). Technologies such as big data, cloud computing, and blockchain can facilitate tracking and monitoring the components of production, thus reducing matching and coordination costs in GVCs (Ferrantino & Koten, 2019) and increasing the efficiency of collaboration across geographies.

To further analyze the relationship between digital technologies and participation in GVCs, we classify technologies according to their role in the process of collecting, analyzing, and exchanging information:

(i) *Data gathering technologies (smart devices and cloud computing).* This category comprises technologies that enable firms to capture, access, and store large amounts of heterogeneous information from multiple sources. These technologies provide SME-EMs with opportunities to develop business resources and capabilities that used to be beyond their reach; for example, cloud computing provides computing resources when they are needed without high fixed costs or initial investment (Chen, Chuang, & Nakatani, 2016). These capabilities may prove essential for the successful integration of SME-EMs in GVCs: smart devices make it possible to collect more and more accurate data (Kos & Kloppenburg, 2019), and cloud computing optimizes applications that rely on large amounts of data (Sturgeon, 2021). Therefore, information that would be otherwise fragmented becomes easily accessible by different players in the value chain (Rejeb et al., 2019). This results in visibility and transparency of information in real time (Strange & Zuchella, 2017), enabling efficient coordination and collaboration throughout the value chain.

(ii) *Data analysis technologies (big data and artificial intelligence).* These technologies are involved in the transformation of information flows and the interpretation of data. Intelligent data processing technologies such as big data analytics, artificial intelligence (AI), and deep learning can process large amounts of data to automate forecasting and decision-making (Sturgeon, 2021), either fully or partially. AI refers to a system that allows firms to interpret and learn from data mimicking a person applying intelligence (Makarius et al., 2020). AI can support decision-making, process automation, and engagement with customers and other stakeholders (Denicolai et al., 2021). Similarly, big data can be used to personalize services and offers, detect failures, and improve agility (Koh et al., 2019). Altogether, data analysis technologies can boost the productivity of firms in emerging markets (Strusani & Houngbonon, 2019), leveraging their analytical capabilities and making more efficient use of their resources. The ability to process big data flows, along with self-learning systems, can support the interaction of SME-EMs with other players involved in GVCs and enhance value chain outcomes in terms of efficiency, flexibility, and profitability (Di Maria et al., 2020).

(iii) *Data sharing technologies (blockchain).* Digital technologies can build trust, traceability, and transparency in GVCs. Blockchain allows transactions to be recorded and verified in a way that is secure from revision and tampering, and shared across all parties engaged in the transaction in an accurate and indisputable manner (Dilyard et al., 2021). Transaction management – traditionally carried out by third-party intermediaries – becomes decentralized, and the use of cryptography ensures the accuracy of information (Chalmers et al., 2021). These technologies support the interoperability among partners involved in GVCs (Rejeb et al., 2019), streamline operations, and improve security and traceability of information flows along the value chain, mitigating risks of network failure (Egwuonwu et al., 2022). This presents distinct opportunities for SME-EMs; by reducing information asymmetries and transaction costs, data sharing technologies can help small businesses overcome challenges regarding scale, opacity, lack of formalization, and reputation and visibility in the market (OECD, 2021). Blockchain can also help bridge any institutional gaps and resolve trust issues that may prevent small businesses in EMs to gain access to GVCs.

Empirical Analysis

Sample

The analysis in this chapter uses data from the Flash Eurobarometer "SMEs, Start-ups, Scale-ups and Entrepreneurship," compiled by the European Commission, Directorate-General for Internal Market, Industry, Entrepreneurship, and SMEs, and coordinated by the Directorate-General for Communication (European Commission, 2020). The survey was administered in 2020 to a sample of both SMEs and larger firms from the 27 European Union (EU) member states and 12 non-EU countries.

Consistently with the focus of this study, we select a sub-sample of 5,966 SMEs[1] from 18 Emerging Markets.[2] We distinguish different types of SMEs by considering micro (<10 employees), small (10–49 employees), and medium (50–249 employees) enterprises. Although SMEs have been traditionally treated as a homogeneous group, there are differences among them (Gherhes et al., 2016; Levenburg, 2005), which may affect the way data-related technologies help them participate in global value chains.

Variables

Dependent variable: Global value chain. Dummy variable which takes value 1 if the firm takes part in a global value chain, and 0 otherwise.

---

1 5,937 observations contain no missing data and are usable for the regression analysis.
2 Bosnia & Herzegovina, Bulgaria, Croatia, Cyprus, Czech Republic, Estonia, Hungary, Kosovo, Latvia, Lithuania, Malta, North Macedonia, Poland, Romania, Serbia, Slovak Republic, Slovenia.

Independent variables. To analyze the different data-related technologies we create three variables: (i) *Data gathering*: dummy variable that takes value 1 if the firm uses cloud computing technologies or smart devices, and 0 otherwise; (ii) *Data analysis*: dummy variable that takes value 1 if the firm uses big data or AI technologies, and 0 otherwise; (iii) *Data sharing*: dummy variable that takes value 1 if the firm uses blockchain technologies, and 0 otherwise.

Control variables. We include additional variables in order to control for firm-specific characteristics, other technologies used, sector, and economic development of a firm's home country. *Firm age*: logarithm of the number of years the firm has been in operation. *Group:* dummy variable that takes value 1 if the firm belongs to a business group, and 0 otherwise. *High speed infrastructure*: dummy variable that takes value 1 if the firm uses basic technologies such as high-speed infrastructures, and 0 otherwise. *Smart manufacturing*: dummy variable that takes value 1 if the company uses if the firm uses robots in its production processes, and 0 otherwise. *GDPpc*: logarithmic transformation of the 2019 GDP per capita in a firm's home country. Finally, we include a set of dummy variables to capture the effects of the industry a firm belongs to.

Methodology and Empirical Results

Given the dichotomous character of the dependent variable, a *probit* model is specified to analyze the relations between the different data-related technologies and the insertion in GVC.

Preliminary Analyses

Table 2.1 provides an overview of the insertion of SME-EMs in GVCs, according to their use of different data-related technologies. Difference-in-proportion tests show that, within our sample, businesses that adopt digital technologies for collecting, analyzing, and sharing data are significantly more likely than other firms to participate in GVCs. For instance, while 5% of observations in our sample participate in GVCs, that proportion reaches 11% for firms using big data or AI technologies, compared to only 3% of those who have not adopted such technologies. These results provide a first indication that SME-EMs may be able to benefit from digital technologies in order to gain access to GVCs.

Table 2.2 displays the descriptive statistics and correlations of the independent and control variables used in this study (with the exception of sector dummies). Descriptive statistics show that the adoption of the different digital technologies is uneven, with data gathering technologies – smart devices and cloud computing – being much more widespread than big data, AI, and blockchain among SME-EMs.

Table 2.1: Use of data-related technologies by global value chain participation.

	Proportion of firms participating in GVCs		
	Use technology	Do not use technology	Difference[a]
Data gathering technologies	0.08	0.03	0.05***
Data analysis technologies	0.11	0.04	0.07***
Data sharing technologies	0.09	0.05	0.04**

[a]One-tailed *t*-tests on the difference between proportions (*p*-values from student's distribution).
p-value: *< 0.05; **< 0.01; ***< 0.001
Note: Proportion of firms participating in GVC (full sample) is 0.05.

Table 2.3 extends these findings by showing that technology usage varies significantly across ranges of firm size (*p*-value < 0.001 for the three types of technologies considered). Unsurprisingly, usage increases monotonically with size; compared to microenterprises, medium-sized businesses are 1.5 times more likely to use data-gathering technologies, twice as likely to use data-analysis technologies, and nearly three times as likely to use data-sharing technologies.

Results

Table 2.4 displays the results of the analysis of the relation between data-related technologies and the participation of the firms in the GVC for the full sample of SME-EMs (model 1), and for the sub-samples corresponding to micro (model 2), small (model 3), and medium (model 4) enterprises.

In the analysis performed on model 1 (SME-EMs full sample), the coefficients for *data gathering technologies* and *data analysis technologies* are both positive and significant; while the coefficient for *data sharing technologies* is negative and nonsignificant. Concerning the micro and small subsamples (models 2 and 3, respectively), both coefficients for *data analysis technologies* are positive and significant, but the effects of *data gathering technologies* are positive and significant only for small firms. The coefficients for *data sharing and monitoring technologies* are nonsignificant across all models. All independent variables are nonsignificant for the subsample of medium firms (model 4).

Discussion and Conclusions

The results we present in this chapter provide compelling evidence suggesting that the use of data-related digital technologies, such as smart sensors, cloud computing, AI, and big data, is associated with participation in GVCs by SMEs from emerging

Table 2.2: Descriptive statistics and correlation matrix.

	Mean	Std. Dev.	1	2	3	4	5	6	7	8	9
Data gathering technologies	0.48	0.50	1.000								
Data analysis technologies	0.15	0.36	0.223***	1.000							
Data sharing technologies	0.02	0.15	0.115***	0.142***	1.000						
Smart manufacturing	0.06	0.24	0.114***	0.163***	0.091***	1.000					
High speed infrastructure	0.23	0.42	0.269***	0.231***	0.119***	0.108***	1.000				
Size	2.10	1.37	0.173***	0.144***	0.054***	0.169***	0.092***	1.000			
Firm age	2.78	0.69	0.028*	-0.002	-0.01	0.011	0.032*	0.271***	1.000		
Group	0.05	0.22	0.079***	0.113***	0.029*	0.080***	0.101***	0.195***	0.020	1.000	
GDP pc 2019	9.65	0.46	0.083***	-0.109***	0.005	0.015	0.075***	-0.007	0.100***	0.025	1.000

*p< 0.05; ** p< 0.01; *** p< 0.001

Table 2.3: Distribution of the data-related technologies used by SMEs in the sample and micro, small, and medium sub-samples.

Data gathering technologies	Micro	Small	Medium	Total SME-EMs
Observed (count)	1492	825	555	2872
Observed (%)	42.3%	52.9%	62.9%	48.1%
Expected (count)	1697	750	425	2872
Pearson Chi-sq: 139.21 d.f. 2 *p*-value <0.001				
Data analysis technologies	**Micro**	**Small**	**Medium**	**Total SME-EMs**
Observed (count)	397	295	206	898
Observed (%)	11.3%	18.9%	23.4%	15.1%
Expected (count)	530	235	133	898
Pearson Chi-sq: 105.42 d.f. 2 *p*-value <0.001				
Data sharing technologies	**Micro**	**Small**	**Medium**	**Total SME-EMs**
Observed (count)	51	45	34	130
Observed (%)	1.4%	2.9%	3.9%	2.2%
Expected (count)	77	34	19	130
Pearson Chi-sq: 24.15 d.f. 2 *p*-value <0.001				
	Micro	**Small**	**Medium**	**Total SME-EMs**
Total observations	3525	1559	882	5966

economies. Odds ratios derived from the empirical models in Table 2.4 show that data gathering – smart sensors and cloud computing – and data analytic – cloud computing and big data – technologies increase the likelihood of SME-EMs participating in GVCs by 34.4% and 38.1%, respectively.

The observed benefits of data technologies are higher for micro and small enterprises, and not significant for medium ones. For example, AI and big data increase the odds of microenterprises participating in GVCs by 53.1%, and sensors and cloud computing have an even greater effect for small businesses (+76.1%). This is consistent with previous research (Chen et al., 2016) and suggests that digitalization may allow the smallest of firms to overcome their resource limitations to cooperate across borders. Meanwhile, medium enterprises, which tend to benefit from more abundant financial and human resources, seem to find paths to access GVCs that do not rely so heavily on advanced data-related technologies.

Table 2.4: Global value chain and data-related technologies for all SME-EMs and the micro, small, and medium sub-samples.

	SME-EMs *Model 1*	Micro *Model 2*	Small *Model 3*	Medium *Model 4*
Data gathering technologies	0.296***	0.147	0.566***	0.252
(cloud & smart devices)	(0.0656)	(0.0927)	(0.127)	(0.155)
Data analysis technologies	0.323***	0.426***	0.386**	−0.0588
(big data & AI)	(0.0735)	(0.114)	(0.128)	(0.163)
Data sharing & monitoring technologies	−0.0355	−0.0794	0.0861	0.0271
(blockchain)	(0.170)	(0.301)	(0.282)	(0.326)
Smart manufacturing	0.178+	0.281	0.148	0.0475
(robots & automatization)	(0.101)	(0.174)	(0.185)	(0.178)
High speed infrastructure	0.207**	0.242*	0.126	0.231
	(0.0668)	(0.101)	(0.120)	(0.145)
Size	0.0802***	0.148*	0.198+	0.171
	(0.0235)	(0.0710)	(0.117)	(0.149)
Firm age	−0.0583	−0.0152	−0.0812	−0.147
	(0.0445)	(0.0641)	(0.0830)	(0.107)
Group	0.799***	0.778***	0.908***	0.843***
	(0.0915)	(0.183)	(0.163)	(0.154)
Industry	Included	Included	Included	Included
GDPpc.	0.0526	0.0262	0.111	0.0303
	(0.0682)	(0.0976)	(0.126)	(0.159)
Intercept	−2.684***	−2.179*	−3.364*	−2.644
	(0.752)	(1.010)	(1.335)	(1.749)
Wald test of full model (χ^2)	272.3***	79.62***	114.2***	60.67***
Log likelihood	−1042.9	−473.0	−326.4	−216.4

Standard errors in parentheses. $^+p < 0.10$. $^*p < 0.05$. $^{**}p < 0.01$, $^{***}p < 0.001$
N = 5937 observations

Unexpectedly, we find that the use of blockchain as a technology for data sharing and monitoring is not significantly linked to participation in GVCs. Recent research has suggested that blockchain can streamline collaboration and lead to value creation in GVCs (Chen et al., 2022; Egwuonwu et al., 2022). However, empirical data show that adoption of blockchain is still limited; only 2.2% of our sample use technology. Altogether, the evidence suggests that, although blockchain may enhance international cooperation and coordination, it is still not a necessary condition for gaining access to GVCs – over 95% of the SME-EMs in our sample that participate in GVCs do not use blockchain. This may change in the near future as the technology becomes progressively more ubiquitous.

There are alternative causal interpretations of the associations we find in our results, which, unfortunately, the cross-sectional nature of the database does not allow to untangle. Whereas we argue that digital technologies equip SMEs to participate in GVCs, the reverse relationship is also plausible: participation in GVCs creates both opportunities and competitive pressures to upgrade business capabilities (Humphrey & Schmitz, 2002); for instance, lead firms may demand that SME-EMs invest in advanced digital technologies as a requirement for them to join the value chain. Both causal interpretations are not mutually exclusive, and may combine into a virtuous cycle, in which digital technologies and internationalization reinforce each other.

References

Brun, L., Gereffi, G., & Zhan, J. (2019). The "Lightness" of Industry 4.0 Lead Firms: Implications for Global Value Chains. In Bianchi, P., Durán, C.R., & Labory, S. (eds.). *Transforming Industrial Policy for the Digital Age*. Edward Elgar Publishing. 37–67. Cheltenham, UK.

Chalmers, D., Matthews, R., & Hyslop, A. (2021). Blockchain as an External Enabler of New Venture Ideas: Digital Entrepreneurs and the Disintermediation of the Global Music Industry. *Journal of Business Research, 125*, 577–591.

Chen, W., Botchie, D., Braganza, A., & Han, H. (2022). A Transaction Cost Perspective on Blockchain Governance in Global Value Chains. *Strategic Change, 31*(1), 75–87.

Chen, T., Chuang, T. T., & Nakatani, K. (2016). The Perceived Business Benefit of Cloud Computing: An Exploratory Study. *Journal of International Technology and Information Management, 25*(4), 101–121.

Denicolai, S., Zucchella, A., & Magnani, G. (2021). Internationalization, Digitalization, and Sustainability: Are SMEs Ready? A Survey on Synergies and Substituting Effects Among Growth Paths. *Technological Forecasting and Social Change, 166*, 120650.

Dilyard, J., Zhao, S., & You, J. J. (2021). Digital Innovation and Industry 4.0 for Global Value Chain Resilience: Lessons Learned and Ways Forward. *Thunderbird International Business Review, 63*(5), 577–584.

Di Maria, E., De Marchi, V., & Galeazzo, A. (2021). Industry 4.0 Technologies and Circular Economy: The Mediating Role of Supply Chain Integration. *Business Strategy and the Environment, 31*(2), 619–632.

Egwuonwu, A., Mordi, C., Egwuonwu, A., & Uadiale, O. (2022). The Influence of Blockchains and Internet of Things on Global Value Chain. *Strategic Change, 31*(1), 45–55.

European Commission (2020). Flash Eurobarometer 486 (SMEs, Start-ups, Scale-ups and Entrepreneurship). GESIS Data Archive, Cologne. ZA7637: Brussels.

Fernández, Z., & Rodríguez, A. (2023). The Value Chain Configuration in the Digital Entrepreneurship Age: The Paradoxical Role of Digital Technologies. In Adams, R.J., Grichnik, D., Pundziene, A., & Volkmann, C. (eds.). *Artificiality and Sustainability in Entrepreneurship. Exploring the Unforeseen and Paving a Way to the Sustainable Future*. Springer, Cham.

Ferrantino, M. J., & Koten, E. E. (2019). Understanding Supply Chain 4.0 and its Potential Impact on Global Value Chains. Global Value Chain Development Report 2019, 103.

Gereffi, G., & Fernandez-Stark, K. (2011). Global Value Chain Analysis: A Primer. Center on Globalization, Governance & Competitiveness, Duke University.

Gherhes, C., Williams, N., Vorley, T., & Vasconcelos, A.C. (2016), Distinguishing Micro-Businesses from SMEs: A Systematic Review of Growth Constraints. *Journal of Small Business and Enterprise Development, 23*(4), 939–963.

Hernández, V., & Pedersen, T. (2017). Global Value Chain Configuration: A Review and Research Agenda. *BRQ Business Research Quarterly, 20*(2), 137–150.

Hosseini, S., Fallon, G., Weerakkody, V., & Sivarajah, U. (2019). Cloud Computing Utilization and Mitigation of Informational and Marketing Barriers of the SMEs from the Emerging markets: Evidence from Iran and Turkey. *International Journal of Information Management, 46*, 54–69.

Humphrey, J., & Schmitz, H. 2002. How Does Insertion in Global Value Chains Affect Upgrading in Industrial Clusters? *Regional Studies, 36*(9), 1017–1027.

Kos, D., & Kloppenburg, S. (2019). Digital Technologies, Hyper-Transparency and Smallholder Farmer Inclusion in Global Value Chains. *Current Opinion in Environmental Sustainability, 41*, 56–63.

Levenburg, N. M. (2005). Does Size Matter? Small Firms' Use of E-business Tools in the Supply Chain. *Electronic Markets, 15*(2), 94–105.

Makarius, E. E., Mukherjee, D., Fox, J. D., & Fox, A. K. (2020). Rising with the Machines: A Sociotechnical Framework for Bringing Artificial Intelligence into the Organization. *Journal of Business Research, 120*, 262–273.

OECD (2021). *The Digital Transformation of SMEs. OECD Studies on SMEs and Entrepreneurship.* OECD Publishing, Paris.

Oliveira, L., Fleury, A., & Fleury, M. T. (2021). Digital Power: Value Chain Upgrading in an Age of Digitization. *International Business Review, 30*(6), 101850.

Opazo-Basáez, M., Vendrell-Herrero, F., Bustinza, O. F., & Marić, J. (2022). Global Value Chain Breadth and Firm Productivity: The Enhancing Effect of Industry 4.0. *Journal of Manufacturing Technology Management, 33*(4), 785–804.

PWC (2016). Industry 4.0: Building the Digital Enterprise. 2016 Global Industry 4.0 Survey.

Rejeb, A., Keogh, J. G., & Treiblmaier, H. (2019). Leveraging the Internet of Things and Blockchain Technology in Supply Chain Management. *Future Internet, 11*(7), 161.

Strange, R., & Zucchella, A. (2017). Industry 4.0, Global Value Chains and International Business. *Multinational Business Review, 25*(3), 174–184.

Strusani, D., & Houngbonon, G.V. (2019). The Role of Artificial Intelligence in Supporting Development in Emerging Markets. EM Compass, 69. International Finance Corporation, World Bank Group.

Sturgeon, T. J. (2021). Upgrading Strategies for the Digital Economy. *Global Strategy Journal, 11*(1), 34–57.

Veile, J. W., Schmidt, M. C., Müller, J. M., & Voigt, K. I. (2021). Relationships Follow Technology! How Industry 4.0 Reshapes Future Buyer-Supplier Relationships. *Journal of Manufacturing Technology Management, 32*(6), 1245–1266.

Wang, J. & Hsu, C. C. (2021), A Topic-Based Patent Analytics Approach for Exploring Technological Trends in Smart Manufacturing. *Journal of Manufacturing Technology Management, 32*(1), 110–135. https://doi.org/10.1108/JMTM-03-2020-0106

Wu, B., & Deng, P. (2020). Internationalization of SMEs from Emerging Markets: An Institutional Escape Perspective. *Journal of Business Research, 108*, 337–350.

Nathalie de Marcellis-Warin, J. Mark Munoz, Hugo Warin,
and Thierry Warin

Chapter 3
Digital Democratization: The Case
of Environmental Risk Management in Haiti

Introduction

New technologies, new data – structured and unstructured – and new ways to analyze these data are appearing at an unprecedented pace. Their reach is broader than ever. For instance, we can use data science approaches to make global supply chains more resilient (Warin, 2022). With the appearance of these new techniques, organizations, private and public, have to consider their future in this new technological context. For governments, it is about becoming a Government 4.0, which means being able to leverage the best technologies to make better public decisions. With the onset of the COVID-19 pandemic, digital transformation has accelerated (De Marcellis-Warin et al., 2020b). It is undeniable that remote work using video-conferencing, instant messaging, and cloud-based document-sharing platforms has seen a higher acceptance level than in past years across organizations (De Marcellis-Warin et al., 2020a). It does not mean, however, that actual digital transformation has taken place. The technologies mentioned existed since the early 2000s. It is about time that its usage be democratized to benefit more people and society in general.

Digital democratization entails a multifaceted engagement. Digital transformation is mostly about data and the artificial intelligence (AI)-based models that manage these data efficiently. It is about installing an AI factory (Iansiti & Lakhani, 2020), coherent multilayered processes and systems that yield results. This is true for private companies, as well as governments (De Marcellis-Warin et al., 2020b).

It comes with some questions: global inequalities and sovereignty questions. At first glance, those technologies are costly to develop and install. Moreover, the business model that seems to create value for these technologies is the platform-based business model. It offers a very centralized infrastructure to the rest of the world. This infrastructure is not expensive to use but expensive to develop. The competitive advantage at the global level comes from development, not usage. This is why the future may see new gaps in terms of economic developments and also some national sovereignty questions.

Now, suppose these concerns are genuine, in particular for developing countries. In that case, it is still possible to use these technologies intelligently or even to propose innovations that might also be used in developed countries, following the pattern of the well-known concept of reverse innovation (Hadengue et al., 2017a, 2017b). Access to digital technologies in many parts of the world, especially in developing nations

https://doi.org/10.1515/9783110734133-003

means that technology can be scaled fairly quickly and can make a considerable impact at the grassroot levels.

This chapter highlights the modalities of digital transformation and democratization that aids in the decision-making process and public policy formation in emerging nations such as Haiti. More precisely, it is about the whole new analytical workflow: (1) generating massive amounts of data; (2) using machine learning (ML) techniques to extract relevant information; and (3) informing and creating effective public policies. Our example is about collecting geographic data using an unmanned aerial vehicle (UAV), analyzing environmental data through ML and informing economic development-oriented public policies in a context of catastrophic disaster risk in Haiti.

Leveling of the Digital Landscape

Far from being science fiction, new technologies enhanced by AI are accessible and often cheap if used in a creative way. A striking example is the case of UAVs, more commonly known as drones. Drones can be used for public policies as a decision-making tool. They can collect geographical data, in all dimensions of the term geography: natural, ecological, human activity, etc., in areas at high risk of natural disasters. There may be no need for the government of one of the least developed countries to invest in a satellite program or to buy the expensive information from a private provider.

Drones have seen their costs going down, providing greater access to this technology. The first uses of drones in research were about mapping the land. For instance, researchers have used drones to map and monitor biodiversity (Wich & Koh, 2018), map mangrove forests (Ruwaimana et al., 2018), or map land movements (Guisado-Pintado, Jackson, & Rogers, 2019). A part of the literature is interested in more economic aspects, but it is still limited to very few domains, such as mining (Kirsch et al., 2018; Suh & Choi, 2017) or agriculture (Puri, Nayyar, & Raja, 2017).

Inspired by a recent trend in the literature about using drones to assess risks in building new civil infrastructures (Ridolfi et al., 2017), and through work experience, the authors decided to use drones to map some parts of Port-au-Prince to measure the urban development in risk areas.

Combined with powerful digital image processing algorithms, drones can be very impactful in terms of risk assessment for three reasons: (1) the quantity of images generated is exponential; (2) the software for processing these images is increasingly powerful and accessible: geographic information systems; and (3) machine learning algorithms and AI offer new information from these images in a significantly inexpensive manner.

These technologies can revolutionize business systems and government programs in emerging nations. It could offer solutions to major societal challenges. For example, could the combination of the three mentioned dynamics impact the management of environmental risks and the potential consequences of natural disasters in developing countries? Very often, environmental risks and economic development are linked. The authors examine the case of Haiti.

Haiti: Environmental Risks, Economic Development, and Natural Catastrophes

With a GDP per capita of approximately US$1176 (*Source:* www.mondo.international 2020), Haiti remains the poorest country in the northern hemisphere and among the world's poorest. With a population of approximately 10 million people, 3 million live in the greater Port-au-Prince area, Haiti's problems are often compounded by urban poverty. In addition to extreme poverty, its geographic location is not conducive to this small country's economic development. This is due to the numerous natural disasters that have struck Haiti in recent years.

Reducing the negative consequences of natural disasters could perhaps already solve part of Haiti's development problem. This became clear, in fact, after 2010. On January 12, 2010, 250,000 people died after just a 35-second earthquake. The natural catastrophe crippled an already weak economy for several years.

Two things were particularly shocking to observe: (1) most of the people who died lived on hill flanks that do not easily allow for solid foundations for their small dwellings and in those districts, and (2) big international organizations would not intervene because of the assumed level of insecurity.

There is an apparent correlation between poor districts and the exposure to the higher consequences of a natural catastrophe such as an earthquake. There is also an evident correlation between the quality of the soil of these poor districts (unstable, soft ground) and the level of risk the population is exposed to. In this context, the proof of concept was to see whether it was possible to map the level of urbanization and the presence/absence of vegetation to stabilize these districts' soil. If the algorithms were able to analyze the difference between houses and vegetation reliably, it would be possible to have a long-term research project that would involve mapping the poor districts through time and measuring the evolution through time of the risk level.

Proliferation of Digital Images

The technological tools of our era make it possible to move in this direction. For this study, a nascent technology was used, the drones. Similar studies focusing on natural disaster response and UAVs exist (Estrada & Ndoma, 2019). Daud et al., (2022) also discussed challenges related to the deployment of drones in mass disasters in the hopes of empowering and inspiring possible future work.

The aim of our research was to make a proof of concept about mapping parts of the large metropolis of Port-au-Prince to facilitate the implementation of public policies in response to natural disasters. Again, this is a simple proof of concept. Although the project was undertaken on a small scale, a large-scale deployment covering the entire metropolis would make it simpler to implement public policies to respond quickly and effectively to the threats of natural disasters in the region while considering economic-oriented urban planning.

Public authorities in developed countries have access to a whole range of sophisticated tools and experts to help them implement responses adapted to their usual problems. When satellite coverage is needed, the United States or Europe can set it up. When world-class analysis platforms and research centers are required, funding can be put in place to achieve these objectives.

The types of questions asked and ways projects are accomplished are quite different in developing countries. The priorities are in other places for obvious reasons. Nevertheless, the fourth industrial revolution offers inexpensive opportunities to access previously unobtainable information for a developing economy. For example, instead of using satellite images, it is now possible to use locally produced images from professional UAVs (Jordan, 2019).

These captured digital images can show many useful elements: the elevation of an area, the quantity, and vegetation's health. Moreover, it is possible to create 3D models with new technologies to assess problems and concerns from different angles. Many software programs are available to analyze these images and uncover new solutions.

Algorithm as an Equalizer

Algorithms have a significant role to play in technological innovation and operational enhancement. Having access to top quality digital images is interesting in itself but analyzing them can be a game-changer. The use of software or geographic information systems (GIS) is already incredibly powerful, and often, the software is available for free. However, it is possible to go even further and use data science and AI techniques. By relying on UAVs' images, AI makes it possible to inform the authorities in a short period of time – sometimes live. For example, the disappearance of an area of vegetation or woodland can significantly impact a shantytown located on a steep slope of a sandy mountainside. The use of drones to analyze forest areas has already been done (Zhang et al., 2016).

During an NGO's humanitarian mission[1] in 2018, the team carried out a proof of concept of mapping by UAV and algorithmic analysis of the data (anonymous). For this proof of concept, they mapped two areas of the metropolis of Port-au-Prince, covering

[1] The NGO *"Ed'Haiti: D'un soleil à l'autre"* was created by Thierry Warin in 2011 after the 2010's earthquake (www.edhaiti.org).

part of Delmas 48 and Emeric. The following images represent approximately 28 hectares of mapping.

Figure 3.1 represents the map of Port-au-Prince and the southern mountainsides.

Figure 3.1: Map of Port-au-Prince.
Source: Google Maps

Here two risk indicators are observable. This chapter will focus on two risk factors: elevation and vegetation. The elevation is considered a mediator, while vegetation is considered a moderator. In what follows, elevation and vegetation presentations are presented as algorithmically determined (Figure 3.2).

Figures 3.3 and 3.4 represent the results of the algorithmic analyses for elevation and (re)vegetation of mountain slopes as an indicator of potential risk. This is indeed just a proof of concept, and further studies are needed to have an accurate measurement of risk. Nevertheless, the low cost of technology and prompt information processing offer significant merit.

Mapping elevation allows public authorities in charge of public safety to create scenarios about the potential consequences of a hazardous event. For instance, public safety authorities can better optimize prevention and intervention activities. In terms of prevention, they can decide to locate first-respondent services better. For intervention in case of an adverse event, they can direct the first respondents to the most impacted locations regarding people or future risks that may cascade from the actual

Figure 3.2: Delmas 48 algorithmically reconstructed in 3D visualization.
Source: Authors' analysis with DroneDeploy software

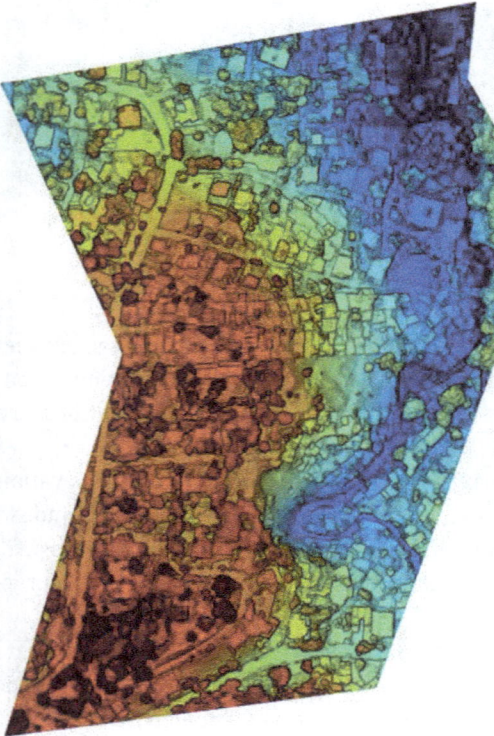

Figure 3.3: Delmas 48's sensitive areas due to their elevation.
Source: Authors' analysis with DroneDeploy software

Figure 3.4: Delmas 48's algorithmic measurement of the presence of vegetation on slopes.
Source: Authors' analysis with DroneDeploy software

event. These scenarios may require other variables, mediating or moderating the risks. For instance, in Figure 3.4, vegetation can play a mediating effect in the case of an earthquake.

Figure 3.5 represents about 18 hectares of mapping, algorithmically reconstructed in 3D visualization.

Figures 3.6 and 3.7 represent the same treatment.

Algorithms have made it possible to obtain quality images and analysis in this emerging nation that is comparable with those in highly developed countries. While the images are extremely helpful in the management of environmental risk, an important question lingers – how can the photos and analyses be scaled throughout the entire country and be used to shape important policy decisions?

Figure 3.5: Emeric algorithmically reconstructed in 3D visualization.
Source: Authors' analysis with DroneDeploy software

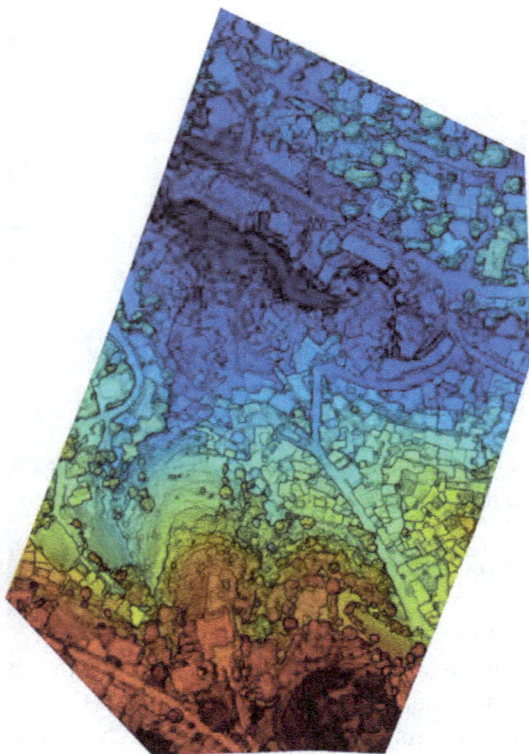

Figure 3.6: Emeric's sensitive areas due to their elevation.
Source: Authors' analysis with DroneDeploy software

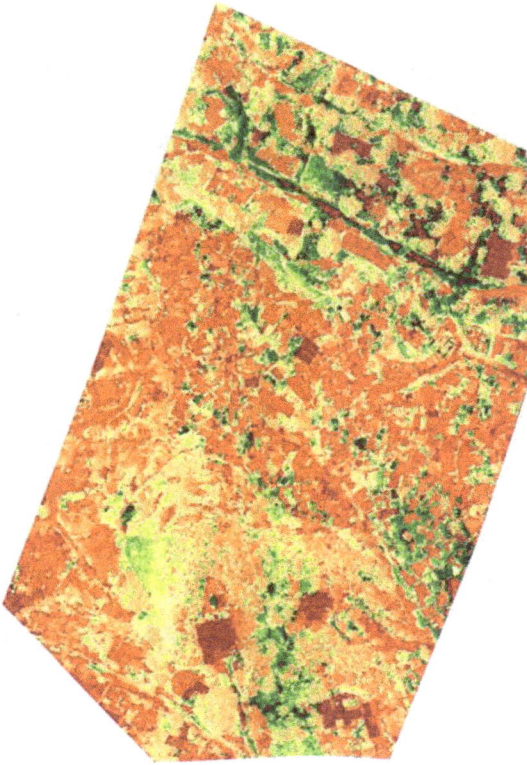

Figure 3.7: Emeric's algorithmic measurement of the presence of vegetation on slopes.
Source: Authors' analysis with DroneDeploy software

Industry and Policy Implications

To answer this question, there are multiple creative ways. The first principle we would like to propose is to think in a multidisciplinary way. Indeed, it should not be the prerogative of one ministry. A second principle is to think of the creation of a public platform. Let us develop a use case. Here, we could imagine providing drones to schools across Haïti. Pupils would develop different abilities and knowledge. To name a few, they would learn how to design a flight plan, their local geography, potential risks, and mitigation plans, and there would be some need for pupils who know how to maintain and repair the drones. This rosy and simplistic example would open up a new world for local schools. At the same time, with the proper governance in place that primarily would be concerned with ethical reasons, some geographical data could be stored on a public platform allowing the right services to have the correct data and analyses to make better decisions. In short, some options may be found if we let people unleash their creativity.

The democratization of digital technologies is taking place worldwide and is opening new doors for countries like Haiti. In this case, the crossover between geographic information systems, robotics (UAVs) and new algorithms (machine learning) can be a source of hope for countries with limited resources and in dire need of valuable information for emergency responses.

This accelerated democratization, however, needs to be accompanied by prompt and strategic decision-making. Supervised and unsupervised machine learning methods, classification systems (machine vector support, empirical Bayesian kriging, k-means, deep learning) combined with new hardware will push the boundaries on how decisions are made in both the private and public sectors.

The rise of the digital era requires governments to embrace new technological perspectives and implement policies in ways never seen before. Governments need to align their systems to unprecedented breadth and scope brought about by digital transformations. In the case of Haiti, it is evident that significant innovations are shattering the silos of the past at an unprecedented speed.

In the spirit of true democracy, equality and opportunity for prosperity brought by new technologies have become accessible to many. The digital tools presently in use in developed nations can be used as a pathway for economic development and societal betterment in developing countries as well.

References

Daud, Sharifah Mastura Syed Mohd, Mohd Yusmiaidil Putera Mohd Yusof, Chong Chin Heo, Lay See Khoo, Mansharan Kaur Chainchel Singh, Mohd Shah Mahmood, Hapizah Nawawi, 2022, Applications of drone in disaster management: A scoping review, *Science & Justice*, Volume 62, Issue 1, Pages 30–42, ISSN 1355-0306. https://doi.org/10.1016/j.scijus.2021.11.002.

De Marcellis N., Munoz, J. M. and Warin T. 2020a "AI in Business: Seeing through the Fog of War", *California Management Review Insights*, https://cmr.berkeley.edu/2020/02/ai-fog-of-war/

De Marcellis-Warin, Nathalie, J. Mark Munoz, & Thierry Warin. 2020b. Government 4.0 and the Pandemic. *California Management Review Insights*. 2020. https://cmr.berkeley.edu/2020/06/government/

Estrada, Mario Arturo Ruiz, & Abrahim Ndoma. 2019. The Uses of Unmanned Aerial Vehicles – UAV's – (or Drones) in Social Logistic: Natural Disasters Response and Humanitarian Relief Aid. Procedia Computer Science, ICTE in Transportation and Logistics 2018 (ICTE 2018), 149 (January), 375–383. https://doi.org/10.1016/j.procs.2019.01.151

Guisado-Pintado, Emilia, Derek W. T. Jackson, & David Rogers. 2019. 3D Mapping Efficacy of a Drone and Terrestrial Laser Scanner over a Temperate Beach-Dune Zone. *Geomorphology*, 328 (March), 157–172. https://doi.org/10.1016/j.geomorph.2018.12.013

Hadengue M., de Marcellis-Warin N., and Warin Th. 2017a. "Reverse Innovation: A Systematic Literature Review" *International Journal of Emerging Markets*, Vol. 12 Issue: 2, pp.142–182, May 2017, DOI: 10.1108/IJoEM-12-2015-0272

Hadengue M., de Marcellis-Warin N., von Zedwitz M. and Warin Th. 2017b. "Avoiding the Pitfalls of Reverse Innovation: Lessons Learned from Essilor" *Research-Technology Management*, Volume 60, Issue 3, pp.40–47 DOI: 10.1080/08956308.2017.1301002

Iansiti, Marco, Karim R. Lakhani. 2020. Competing in the Age of AI. *Harvard Business Review*, January 1, 2020. https://hbr.org/2020/01/competing-in-the-age-of-ai

Jordan, B., 2019. Collecting field data in volcanic landscapes using small UAS (sUAS)/drones, *Journal of Volcanology and Geothermal Research*, Volume 385, Pages 231–241,ISSN 0377-0273,https://doi.org/10.1016/j.jvolgeores.2019.07.006.

Kirsch, Moritz, Sandra Lorenz, Robert Zimmermann, Laura Tusa, Robert Möckel, Philip Hödl, René Booysen, Mahdi Khodadadzadeh, & Richard Gloaguen. 2018. "Integration of Terrestrial and Drone-Borne Hyperspectral and Photogrammetric Sensing Methods for Exploration Mapping and Mining Monitoring." *Remote Sensing*, 10(9), 1366. https://doi.org/10.3390/rs10091366

Puri, Vikram, Anand Nayyar, and Linesh Raja. 2017. Agriculture Drones: A Modern Breakthrough in Precision Agriculture. *Journal of Statistics and Management Systems*, 20(4),507–518. https://doi.org/10.1080/09720510.2017.1395171

Ridolfi, Elena, Giulia Buffi, Sara Venturi, & Piergiorgio Manciola. 2017. Accuracy Analysis of a Dam Model from Drone Surveys. *Sensors*, 17(8), 1777. https://doi.org/10.3390/s17081777

Ruwaimana, Monika, Behara Satyanarayana, Viviana Otero, Aidy M. Muslim, Muhammad Syafiq A, Sulong Ibrahim, Dries Raymaekers, Nico Koedam, & Farid Dahdouh-Guebas. 2018. The Advantages of Using Drones over Space-Borne Imagery in the Mapping of Mangrove Forests. *PLOS ONE*, 13(7),e0200288. https://doi.org/10.1371/journal.pone.0200288

Suh, Jangwon, & Yosoon Choi. 2017. Mapping Hazardous Mining-Induced Sinkhole Subsidence Using Unmanned Aerial Vehicle (Drone) Photogrammetry. *Environmental Earth Sciences*, 76(4), 144. https://doi.org/10.1007/s12665-017-6458-3

Warin, T. (2022). "Supply chains under pressure: How can data science help?" (2022PE-06, CIRANO). https://doi.org/10.54932/NJYX4623

Wich, Serge A., & Lian Pin Koh. 2018. *Conservation Drones: Mapping and Monitoring Biodiversity*. Oxford University Press, Oxford. Online edn, Oxford Academic, 23 Aug. 2018, https://doi.org/10.1093/oso/9780198787617.003.0005, accessed 24 Mar. 2023.

Zhang, J., Jianbo Hu, Juyu Lian, Zongji Fan, Xuejun Ouyang, Wanhui Ye. 2016. Seeing the forest from drones: Testing the potential of lightweight drones as a tool for long-term forest monitoring, *Biological Conservation*, Volume 198, Pages 60–69, ISSN 0006-3207, https://doi.org/10.1016/j.biocon.2016.03.027.

RJ Podeschi
Chapter 4
IOT in Tourism

Introduction

Internet-enabled devices have found their way into the modern vacation as a way to reduce friction for guests while gathering valuable data that can be used for creating targeted marketing campaigns and improving operational efficiencies. Organizations continually seek competitive advantages through digitization and system automation. These are often achieved through large enterprise systems that manage customer relationships and supply chains. In particular, radio frequency identification (RFID) has been at the forefront of tracking materials and products both upstream and downstream through the supply chain. RFID uses electronic tags, in combination with a reader, to identify objects wirelessly over short distances (Baltzan, 2016) and is considered to be part of the Internet of Things (IoT) category. While several efficiencies have been gained through the use of RFID technology, the technology has been successful in several other contexts such as: door security, contactless payments, timing road races, and logging tollway charges. The global RFID market size was approximately $17 billion in 2018 and is forecast to grow to just over $26 billion by 2025 (360iResearch, 2020).

More recently, The Walt Disney Company, a recognized leader in entertainment, theme park experiences, and technology, launched a $1 billion initiative in 2013 to transform the theme park experience through MyMagic+ system that uses RFID technology (Lev-Ram, 2014), a mobile application, ubiquitous Wi-Fi, and other IoT devices. This system transforms the way guests experience the Disney resorts and theme parks by seamlessly integrating their online account with their theme park tickets, attraction selections, dining, and payment processing. All of this reinforces Disney's "Keys to the Kingdom," their standards for excellent guest service, consisting of safety, courtesy, show, and efficiency. This chapter explores the use of IoT, RFID technology specifically, to improve the guest experience and achieve operational efficiencies at the famed Orlando resort, and how Disney has paved the way for other players in the tourism industry.

History of RFID

RFID is an established technology and has been available in similar forms since its first use in World War II when transponders were used to identify whether aircraft was friend or foe. RFID technology works on the same principle as World War II fighters where a signal is sent to a transponder, which then either returns back a signal or

https://doi.org/10.1515/9783110734133-004

broadcasts its own signal with a small and lightweight RFID chip. RFID usage began in the 1960s, but didn't accelerate until the 1970s. In the late 1960s, electronic article surveillance (EAS) tags were developed. EAS tags were arguably the first and most widespread commercial use of RFID. Two formats existed; the single-bit EAS tag and the multi-bit EAS tag. While single-bit EAS tags were relatively small, multi-bit tags were the size of a loaf of bread, constrained in size by the dictates of the circuitry (Landt, 2005). By 1978, RFID tags had improved with reductions in size and became more functional. The key to these advancements was the use of low-voltage, low power logic circuits (Landt, 2005). Through research and development over the years, the tags continued to shrink and become more functional. Even though the tags were becoming smaller in size over time, they still remained expensive for several years.

The three components that make up an RFID system include an antenna coil, a transceiver with a decoder, and a transponder (more commonly known as a "tag") which includes the unique identification number. Transponders can either be passive or active. Passive transponders do not contain a power supply or battery and are activated by the transceiver signal. (Deal, 2004). Newer versions use UHF transmission that can store either 4 or 8 kilobytes of data (RFID Journal, n.d.). Active transponders are able to transmit data over large distances with the assistance of a power supply and have the ability to read and write data (Deal, 2004).

RFID technology is mainly used in applications where tags are interacting with each other automatically to exchange information. RFID tags use radio frequency waves for exchanging information between one another without line of sight or physical contact. It uses the wireless technology of automatic identification and data capture (AIDC) (Borgohain, et al., 2015). These tags are small microchips made of silicon and can be as small as a half millimeter square. The transistor stores a unique serial number and additional information and is read wireless, by readers, from a few inches to several hundred feet (Taghaboni-Dutta & Velthouse, 2006, p. 65). The reader is a specialized combined radio transmitter and receiver that sends out a signal that the tags are programmed to, and respond to, by sending the unique data programmed into the tag (Deal, 2004, p. 24). Signaling between the tag and the reader is done using multiple methods depending on the frequency band used by the tag. Tags can be read if passed near a reader, even if the tag is not visible or covered by another object, and readers are capable of reading hundreds of tags simultaneously (Vogler, 2015).

Walt Disney World Launches MyMagic+

While RFID tags have been successful in managing the supply chain, speeding up tollways, and timing a local 5K race more efficiently, the technology continues to be repurposed for innovative use cases. In 2013, The Walt Disney Company rolled out a new product in their Orlando, Florida, theme parks called MyMagic+. With a $1 billion price tag and a team of over 1,000 cast members, the integrated system utilized a rubber, waterproof wristband with an embedded RFID tag that acted as a guest's "key to the world" (Kuang, 2015). The band uses both 13.56 MHz and 2.4 GHz frequencies to accommodate both short and long-range reads respectively (Swedberg, 2014). During an 18-month implementation, Disney replaced 283 ticket turnstiles and over 28,000 resort rooms, in addition to countless point-of-sale terminals and related devices (Kuang, 2015; Swedberg, 2014). The MagicBand can be used for theme park entry, resort room access, scheduled attraction entry known as FastPass+, electronic payment for food and souvenirs, digital photographs through a service known as PhotoPass, and other uses to add to the guest experience.

Disney integrated their RFID-enabled MagicBands with mobile and web applications called My Disney Experience that allows the guest to customize their vacation from the point of booking to the time they return home. Guests have the ability to consult the mobile app in the theme parks to get up-to-date wait times, adjust Fast-Passes, make dining reservations, and view park maps. Disney's $1 billion investment included installing resort-wide Wi-Fi that is free to guests, thereby decreasing network latency to their mobile applications and conserving precious cellular data.

Improving Guest Experiences through RFID

The Walt Disney Company, under the leadership of Bob Iger, found an innovative method for using RFID in the resort and theme park settings. One year after launching the new system, Disney saw a 50% increase in FastPass+ participation over the paper ticket method and wait times have decreased by 25% on average (Fast Company, 2014). Through this technology, Disney has been able to improve the guest experience by allowing the "magic to happen" by removing barriers, perceived or actual. For example, guests can order a meal at a counter service restaurant and have it delivered to their table based on the location of their MagicBand in the dining room. The thousands of RFID sensors and the 100 systems linked together to create MyMagic+ turn the park into a giant computer – streaming real-time data about where guests are, what they're doing, and what they want (Kuang, 2015). By implementing technology seamlessly into the Disney ecosystem, the company can be even more intentional about putting guests first.

Walt Disney's principles of establishing a brand reputation for outstanding customer service continues to drive repeat business (James, 2013). McKinsey and Company established the customer decision journey to illustrate how a consumer goes through four phases of the "brand loyalty loop." Initially, the consumer is introduced to multiple brands through perceptions and exposure to touch points. Next, the consumer adds or subtracts brands as they are actively evaluating their choices. Ultimately, the consumer selects a brand and builds expectations following the purchase to become a repeat customer (Court et al., 2009). Disney excels at the loyalty loop by engaging the guest long before their vacation begins (when they book their trip), while on Disney property, and long after they have returned home (browsing and purchasing photos) through the My Disney Experience application. Furthermore, customized campaigns through email or social media can be used through the harvesting of data gathered from the MagicBand.

The MagicBand system compliments My Disney Experience by gathering and harnessing the power of the guest's data, which ranges from purchasing habits to favorite attractions. Through business intelligence, Disney now has the capability to target individual guests or a population of guests with similar attributes for repeat visits through promotions. Additionally, data mining techniques can be used to predict guest behavior or theme park crowd patterns by using RFID reads at attractions or through long-range readers throughout the theme parks. Push notifications can be sent through the mobile app to redirect crowds to empty areas of the park. After the implementation of the MagicBand system, Disney was able to support 3,000 additional guests during their peak holiday season (Palmeri, 2014). The MagicBand system has not only improved guest experience and repeat visitors, but has also driven operational efficiencies.

Privacy Concerns and Implementation Issues

The implementation of the MagicBand system has not been entirely perfect. Privacy over data gathered from scanning RFID tags has been at the forefront of the conversation. While Disney can certainly profit from integrating the MyMagic+ data into their customer relationship management systems, concern over how that data is handled, and, in particular, for data gathered on children. In January 2013, a scathing letter was sent to Disney Chairman Bob Iger by Massachusetts Congressman Edward Markey stating the technology recklessly or haphazardly manipulates and places the children's safety at risk. Chairman Iger responded by citing the company's privacy policy and defended the program by assuring that Disney does not personalize advertisements or share children's information with third parties (Markey, 2013). The MyMagic+ system is optional, and guests have control over their RFID bands and data through the My Disney Experience app. While institutional data gathered from RFID-tagged objects for product tracking in the supply chain is rather benign, the concern level is heightened as RFID technology has become integrated into wearable technology, as in the MyMagic+ system.

Although Disney spent over three years in development, months in testing, and implemented the system in carefully phased in approach over 18 months, loyal Disney World guests had a difficult time adjusting to the new MyMagic+ system as they had already mastered the old paper-based FastPass system. New guests were slightly confused despite all of the literature, videos, and email communication used to instruct how the technology was to be used in the parks. Because of the implementation of the MyMagic+ system, guest behavior needed to evolve based on their preconceived notion on how theme parks operated. Quickly, through Disney's outstanding guest service, park attendees recognized the benefits and efficiencies of the RFID technology as if it really was all magic.

MyMagic+ Evolution

Since 2013, Walt Disney continues to tweak the program. For example, as of 2016, guests can now modify and add FastPass+ selections from their mobile device in the park where this previously had to be completed at a designated kiosk. New uses for the long-range 2.4 GHz transponder have been added over time as guests now receive customized goodbye messages at the end of the It's a Small World boat attraction and PhotoPass photos are automatically linked to your account when taken on attractions like Seven Dwarves Mine Train and Expedition Everest.

Disney has built an infrastructure that has capacity for future enhancements. For example, long-range readers could theoretically count guests as they leave the theme park at the end of the day to match them up with their resort. Predictive analytics could then be used to determine how many buses, monorails, and boats are needed to transport guests back to their resorts. This has the potential for improving the guest experience by minimizing the wait for an available bus while also reducing the cost of transportation.

In 2020, Walt Disney World responded to the global coronavirus pandemic and implemented several measures to protect the health and safety of guests while remaining operational in reduced capacity. The MagicBand RFID system has allowed Disney to implement a park reservation system (similar to FastPass+) for each theme park, manage reduced park capacity levels, and conduct contact tracing when necessary. With the infrastructure in place, the Walt Disney Company can continue to maximize its return on investment by leveraging the data gathered from MagicBands improving guest service through new features.

Other Tourism Applications

Disney's has greatly improved the guest experience through their intentional focus on creative uses for IoT devices such as the MagicBand. This new way of using RFID technology is changing the way other organizations' processes are accomplished and is increasing the efficiency and profitability of the organization as a result.

Other organizations are beginning to use RFID technology outside of traditional use cases to improve their customers' experience. Airlines have deployed RFID baggage tracking technology to provide customers with improved real-time tracking of luggage throughout the travel experience (Morrow, 2016a). Customers are able to see where their luggage is on a map through a mobile app, and receive live push notifications from critical points along their bags' journey. (Morrow, 2016b). The Transportation Security Administration (TSA) is expanding its deployment of RFID-enabled baggage screening technology at U.S. airports. The technology has proven to increase passenger-screening efficiency by 30% (Swedberg, 2016). Furthermore, border patrol agencies are now integrating RFID chips into passports for electronic verification at border checkpoints. When combined with other internet-enabled technologies like biometrics and video surveillance, additional security measures can be implemented to curtail wanted criminals from crossing international lines.

RFID systems are also finding their ways into more tourism companies. Ski resorts, like those in famed Vail, Colorado, are using RFID tags embedded in ski lift tags to count uses, govern entry times, and control crowds. TopGolf, a chain of golf entertainment facilities, employs RFID tags embedded in golf balls. There are 500 RFID readers in the driving range that form various zones. When a golf ball falls into a zone, the readers scan its RFID chip, and the data is passed back to the Topgolf system to register the score (Brousell, 2015).

Due to the decrease in size and cost of RFID technology, additional uses will continue to be developed through creative innovation. As more objects contain embedded RFID tags, data privacy and security will continue to be at the forefront of the conversation. Organizations will continue to look at RFID and other technology-related solutions that help increase revenue, improve operational efficiency, and keep customers engaged in their brand.

Discussion and Conclusions

IoT technologies like RFID have been making their way into innovative uses in tourism over the past decade. While tourism-oriented companies were motivated to implement these technologies to drive revenue, increase efficiencies, and improve the experience, many are finding creative uses for these applications to assist with mitigating the spread of infectious diseases and aid in contact tracing. The technology couldn't have been timelier as society will need these tools to live in a post-pandemic world. We may very well begin to see vaccine information loaded to RFID cards or embedded in other wearable technologies to allow for the safe passage within and between countries. Regardless, the tourism industry has benefited from this technology and it may be one of the keys to aid in their recovery from a global pandemic.

References

[360]iResearch. (2020, March). Global RFID Market Size, Share, Trends, and Forecast 2025. Retrieved from https://reports.valuates.com/market-reports/360I-Auto-3Y72/rfid-market

At Disney World, the fun never stops. (2014). *Fast Company* (189), 132–133.

Baltzan, Paige. 2016. *Business Information Systems, 5e*. New York: McGraw-Hill.

Borgohain, T., Kumar, U., & Sanyal, S. (2015, January 9). Survey of Security and Privacy Issues of Internet of Things. *ARXIV*. Retrieved from https://arxiv.org/abs/1501.02211

Brousell, L. (2015, August 8). *Inside Look at Topgolf's High Tech Driving Ranges*. Retrieved from http://www.cio.com/article/2974192/consumer-technology/inside-look-at-topgolfs-high-tech-driving-ranges.html

Court, D., Elzinga, D., Mulder, S., & Vetvik, O. J. (2009). The Consumer Decision Journey. *McKinsey Quarterly*. Retrieved from https://www.mckinsey.com/capabilities/growth-marketing-and-sales/our-insights/the-consumer-decision-journey

Deal, I. F. (2004). RFID: A Revolution in Automatic Data Recognition. *Technology Teacher, 63*(7), 23–27.

James, J. (2013, January 5). The Heart Makes the Mouse: Disney's Approach to Brand Loyalty. *Journal of Brand Strategy, 2*(1), 16–20.

Kuang, C. (2015, March 10). Disney's $1 Billion Bet on a Magical Wristband. Wired.

Landt, J. (2005). The History of RFID. *IEEE Potentials, 24*(4), 8–11. doi:10.1109/MP.2005.1549751

Lev-Ram, M. (2014, December 29). Empire of Tech. *Fortune, 171*(1), 48–58.

Markey, Edward J. (2013), Letter to Robert A. Iger. https://insidethemagic.net/2013/01/disney-ceo-bob-iger-sternly-replies-to-congressman-markeys-letter-addressing-magicband-privacy-concerns/

Morrow, A. (2016a, April 28). *Delta Introduces Innovative Baggage Tracking Process*. Retrieved from http://news.delta.com/delta-introduces-innovative-baggage-tracking-process

Morrow, A. (2016b, November 15). *Fly Delta app Push Notifications take stress Out of Checking a Bag*. Retrieved from Delta: http://news.delta.com/fly-delta-apppush-notifications-take-stress-out-checking-bag

Palmeri, C. (2014, March 7). Disney Bets $1 Billion on Technology to Track Theme-Park Visitors. Bloomberg Businessweek. Retrieved from http://www.businessweek.com/articles/2014-03-07/disney-bets-1-billion-on-technology-to-track-theme-park-visitors

RFID Journal. (n.d.). *RFID Frequently Asked Questions*. Retrieved from https://www.rfidjournal.com/faq/show?66

Swedberg, C. (2014, June 16). *MagicBands Bring Convenience, New Services to Walt Disney World*. RFID Journal. Retrieved from http://www.rfidjournal.com/articles/view?11877/

Swedberg, C. (2016, July 18). *TSA Hopes to RFID-enable 60 Security Lanes This Year*. RFID Journal. Retrieved from http://www.rfidjournal.com/articles/view?14744

Taghaboni-Dutta, F., & Velthouse, B. (2006). RFID Technology Is Revolutionary: Who Should Be Involved in this Game of Tag? *Academy Of Management Perspectives, 20*(4), 65–78. doi:10.5465/AMP.2006.23270307

Vogler, K. (2015, August 21). *RFID Over Wi-Fi*. Tech First Magazines. Retrieved from https://www.technologyfirst.org/magazines/2015/21-august/1065-rfid-over-wi-fi.html

Aldo Alvarez-Risco, Agnieszka Olter, and Shyla Del-Aguila-Arcentales

Chapter 5
Internet of Things and Smart Cities as Accelerators for International Business

Introduction

International business is a business that takes place across boarders (Stobierski, 2021). The digital transformation facilitated by Internet of Things (IoT) might positively impact many aspects of international business (Lundan, 2018). The rising pervasiveness of the IoT, based on digital solutions, presents a multitude of emerging business opportunities and new business models comprising a network of partners (Turber et al., 2014). IoT is an extensive system of devices with unique identifiers that cooperate by exchanging data and creating new insights (Firouzi et al., 2020). Within that shared network, there are computers and mobile devices like tablets and smartphones, as well as others that possess a sensor, like wearable technology devices or autos. IoT differs from other currently expanding solutions like the machine to machine communication (M2M) due to the fact that it uses diverse communications protocols, requires an active internet connection, and gives various integration options (Firouzi et al., 2020). IoT exists within a broad environment composed not just of things (devices), but also data, people, and processes (Maksimovic, 2018).

A smart city uses information and communication technologies to build intelligent and digital cities to improve citizens' quality of life (Garg et al., 2017; Tabaa et al., 2020). It uses connected devices to collect data, analyze it, and provide feedback to improve the management of services and resources (Zanella et al., 2014). Furthermore, a smart, sustainable city focuses on boosting the efficiency of urban settings and the city's competitiveness and ensures meeting the needs of current citizens without undermining future generations' possibilities to do the same. It thus aims at focusing on the city's economic, social, and environmental sustainability (Salem et al., 2020). The challenge for the smart city is in building an appropriate infrastructure for the IoT, as it requires a complex system of devices and technologies to work together seamlessly (Khan et al., 2020). Moreover, a smart city design incorporates smart citizens who shall receive proper education to design, fully participate, and capitalize on technological solutions (Williamson, 2015). The study will review how international business may be affected due to the growing use of IoT and the rising presence of smart cities around the world.

https://doi.org/10.1515/9783110734133-005

International Business: Current Situation

The global economy is still under threat as a consequence of the wave of lockdowns due to the COVID-19 pandemic. In that uncertain period, the role of technology, the IoT, and artificial intelligence (AI) is fundamental to recover and ensure economic prosperity in the "new normality" of the post-COVID-19 era (Lee & Lee, 2021). Digital technologies, like IoT, big data, or robotics systems have great impact on international business (Ghauri et al., 2021). The new digital technologies can potentially disrupt the global value chains (GVCs) as well as redefine where specific activities are located and how they are organized. Even though Industry 4.0 is still in its initial life stage, it has already impacted the character of competition and business strategies in several industries, which shows its potential to reorganize the international business (Strange & Zucchella, 2017).

Technology has a great potential to boost innovation and improve people's lives. If used effectively, it may become a source of competitive advantages for companies (Yu & Zhang, 2019). Lately, the big data from IoT leveraged by digital technology has disrupted the way business is made, opening tremendous opportunities for international business (Ghauri et al., 2021). The new reality, brought by the COVID-19 pandemic, accelerated companies' adoption of IoT and digital tools. Many businesspeople affirm that most of their interactions with customers occur via digital channels, and internal operations, such as supply chain, production, and R&D, went much more digital (McKinsey & Company, 2020).

Smart Cities

Concept of Smart City

Authors have different understandings of smart cities. Most agree they constitute a combination of smart people, technology, and are based on collaboration (Meijer & Bolívar, 2015); however, others include smart economy, governance, mobility, environment, and even living (Vienna University of Technology, 2017). The smart city unites information and communication technology (ICT) and numerous physical appliances that join the IoT network to enhance the performance of city services and processes while closely related to citizens (Ahad et al., 2020). Smart cities are characterized by technological, policy, and management innovation (Visvizi et al., 2018), which allow real-time responses (Barthélemy et al., 2019; Rathore et al., 2018). Another relevant component of a smart city is IoT, which allows employing advanced technologies to create enhanced services for citizens (Zanella et al., 2014).

Opportunities of Smart Cities in International Business

The remaining and challenging task for the city governors is to demonstrate to citizens that smart cities can produce and sustain value (Díaz-Díaz et al., 2017; Walravens, 2012). Like the Business Model Canvas, often used by firms to prove how the value is created for the customers, the city business model may explain how smart cities will create value for the citizens (Ben Letaifa, 2015). Smart cities require modern decision-making models based on improved government capabilities and synergetic and collaborative systems (Schaffers et al., 2011). Policy makers and local governments need to analyze and demonstrate smart cities' economic, social, and environmental costs and benefits. The city model canvas serves as a framework for designing smart cities, whose performance, economic viability, social inclusiveness, and environmental sustainability should then be assessed (Timeus et al., 2020).

The Fourth Industrial Revolution, or Industry 4.0., fundamentally transforms the way companies manufacture and distribute their products. Its elements as IoT, cloud computing, artificial intelligence (AI), machine learning, blockchain, and business analytics, revolutionize global lives and change business-as-usual practices (Zhang & Chen, 2019). Manufacturers integrate these new technologies, within their value chain, as increasing automation, and smart factories allow them to work more productively and boost efficiency (IBM, 2021). That, in turn, helps to plan optimally, enhance risk management, enable new products and services, and as a consequence bring more profitability (Pérez-Pons et al., 2021). Improved monitoring of processes and systems makes workers safer (Li & Parlikad, 2016). IoT also is fundamental for addressing global hurdles like climate change (Carr & Lesniewska, 2020), contamination (Harshitha et al., 2021), and epidemics (Chamola et al., 2020; Singh et al., 2020).

One of the most prominent examples of the IoT business application is within supply chain management, as it allows actors to connect through internet networks (Ben-Daya et al., 2019; Jagtap et al., 2021). The supply chain is an arrangement of the activities needed to produce and deliver goods or services (Mentzer et al., 2001). One of the crucial problems in the supply chain is delays in getting information, which leads to nonadequate inventory, high logistics cost, and loss in revenue (Schmid et al., 2013). IoT-enabled supply chain integrates communication technologies, connects suppliers and distributors and available resources through internet (de Vass et al., 2021), and provides the data at the right moment to minimize potential threats and prevent delays (Parry et al., 2016). That changes the operating mode of supply chain management (Min et al., 2019), increasing its efficiency (Dehgani & Jafari Navimipour, 2019) by overcoming such challenges as uncertainty, complexity, and price (Zong et al., 2020), providing a systematic approach to supply chains (Accorsi et al., 2017). As a consequence, customer requirements are better satisfied (Mostafa et al., 2019).

Optimizations that emerge from the data-rich environment allowed by IoT save time, money, and energy, improving quality of life and overall well-being (Firouzi et al., 2020). IoT gives clients the capacity to make more informed decisions (Deloitte,

2021); however, IoT also brings possible disadvantages, like a transgression of privacy (Deloitte, 2021), over-reliance on technology (Rainie & Anderson, 2017), and the unprecedented loss of jobs (Schwab, 2016). Technology readiness describes individuals' capacity, willingness, and confidence to use new technologies (Parasuraman, 2000). It also exhibits customers' inclination to accept or decline a new technological solution (Rosenbaum & Wong, 2015). While confidence and enthusiasm are recognized as enablers that strengthen an individual's propensity to embrace new technology, discomfort and doubtlessness cause its resisting or rejection (Roy et al., 2018).

In Spanish city Santander, the adjusted business model was put into practice. Various urban intelligent services based on smart processes and the IoT technology were implemented in the management of water, waste, traffic, street lighting, or tourism, which allowed reducing energy consumption and lowered costs, having a positive long-term environmental and social impact (Díaz-Díaz et al., 2017). Three smart services developed within the quintuple helix in the city of Santander are analyzed:

- Waste management: Implementation of sensors to provide information on the status of containers boosted service efficiency as it allowed for the replacement of existing predefined routes with new ones defined according to the location of full containers. A mobile application informed residents about the fill of containers, the recollection routes, and schedules, making them active participants and further enhancing the service's efficiency. The city council, the University of Cantabria, and the service provider collaborated to implement that innovation. The canvas model showed how the smart service based on IoT reduced cost and limited environmental pollution.
- Water supply: The Smart Water project was implemented based on the collaboration of the city government, the University of Cantabria, and the company FCC Aqualia as a service provider. Its main goal was to introduce an effective detection system, which would reduce water leakage, as it represented approximately 20% of the total amount of water displaced in water networks. The sensors introduced within the water distribution network measured water pressure and its quality parameters, allowing quick detection of the leakage source and instantly sending information about the needed repair.
- Traffic management: Since transport in the European Union accounts for roughly 30% of the whole energy consumptions and 27% of the accumulated greenhouse gas emissions (Falvo et al., 2011), while collisions and traffic constitute a considerable budgetary burden (Haque et al., 2013), optimization of traffic management is crucial for energy-saving, strengthening the sustainability and improving life quality (High-level Advisory Group on Sustainable Transport, 2016). In Santander, a traffic light and parking spot management system based on smart sensors was implemented, enabling instantaneous responses to changing conditions and thus enhancing urban traffic management. A mobile application, which gave information on traffic situations in real-time, was provided so that citizens could pick the fastest routes. Optimization of urban traffic, based on IoT, resulted in reduced energy consumption and environmental impact and enhanced resident satisfaction (Vlahogianni et al., 2016).

IoT

Having millions of devices connected to the Internet means that the generation of data (and its storage) multiplies exponentially. This has important implications, since it involves what we know as Big Data: data from thousands of devices and sensors ready to be processed for a specific purpose. For example, the IoT makes possible the smart home, smart cities and allows the digitization of production chains in factories to optimize performance and save costs, among other things.

Concept of IoT

The IoT does not just capture and share data; it processes and acts on it, which, in turn, informs savvy decisions concerning issues like industrial processes or business arrangements (Almeida et al., 2020). IoT has entered different fields of human activity as:

a. Logistics: Radio frequency identification (RFID) tags placed on suppliers' packages and trays (Popova et al., 2021); real-time monitoring and optimization of conditions during storage and transportation (Alfian et al., 2017; Ding et al., 2018)

b. Agriculture: Environmental monitoring and remote diagnosis system for plant diseases (García-Berná et al., 2020; Jia et al., 2021)

c. Petroleum: The real-time energy data provided by a wireless sensor help to decide on the best time to get the energy (Aba et al., 2021)

d. Utilities: Technology enables lower energy use in buildings (Ahad et al., 2020).

e. Lifestyle: Smart homes adjust chosen features according to user's needs and external conditions; smart waste management (Furszyfer Del Rio et al., 2020; Nicholls et al., 2020).

f. Healthcare: Sensors collect and examine the patients' data, allowing doctors to respond appropriately (Farahani et al., 2020; Haghi Kashani et al., 2021)

Opportunities of Smart Cities in International Business

Only seven decades ago, in 1950, less than 30% of the world's population lived in cities (Firouzi et al., 2020). The United Nations (2018) claims that by 2050, that number might grow to as much as 68%. By 2030, there will be 43 megacities, that is, these that comprise more than 10 million citizens, the vast majority of them in developing countries. Megacities tend to not grow organically, and many challenges arise due to the lack of proper urban planning and design (United Nations, 2018). Additionally, food production will need to increase by 60% by 2050 to satisfy global demands in the face of possible disruptions like pandemics and a growing population. Therefore, there is an increasing need to transform the farming methods with technology, enhancing productivity and securing food production, for instance, by applying urban smart vertical farming (Saad et al., 2021).

As the number of residents rises, it puts huge pressure on the local environment. The growing amount of energy, food, and other products consumed and waste that the local government must remove from the city challenges the transportation system and the city itself. The cities are responsible for the consumption of approximately 60–80% of the energy used on our planet, contributing significantly to greenhouse gas emissions. Urban areas consume 60% of potable water globally, out of which an estimated 20% is wasted in leakage. It is essential to use of these critical resources more efficiently (Hashem et al., 2016). Nowadays, in many cities, services are not interdependent; and no significant collaboration is achieved, which causes waste and deficiencies in meeting citizens' needs. That is why an optimized city management system is needed, based on IoT and smart solutions to solve the urban areas' inefficiencies (Firouzi et al., 2020). The IoT in smart cities can be used in multiple ways, including devices that enable to collect and analyze that triggers automated actions. That data can be useful for city management to find opportunities to optimize utilities, water supply, power plants, check the status of waste removal, or improve the transportation systems and parking arrangement. Also, law enforcement can benefit from the smart systems to verify whether tools were paid or may even help detect crime (Firouzi et al., 2020). Also, institutions like schools and hospitals and private citizens can benefit (Agyeman & McLaren, 2017).

Example of Smart City: Case Taiwan

Smart cities build based on IoT and, with a sustainable approach, improve citizens' quality of life and enhance the city's competitiveness (Wu et al., 2018). Several urban areas in Taiwan are acknowledged by several ratings, among them as European Smart City Index (City Keys, 2016), Intelligent Community Awards (Intelligent Community Forum, 2021), Smart City China (2021), Foreseeing Innovative New Digi Services (2021). Tainan city was selected as one of the 2018 Top 7 Intelligent Communities by the Intelligent Community Forum (ICF). The city management aspires to set an innovative and people-oriented environment based on modern technological solutions. Some of the solutions are listed below (Hsiao et al., 2021):

- Connectivity: Broadband services' coverage has already reached 95%. To maximize public safety, 24 million beacon microlocation services were installed (Ji et al., 2015). Beacons also help to provide traffic and parking navigation (Chien et al., 2020; Handscombe & Yu, 2019) and improve tourist experience (Gonçalves et al., 2019).
- Energy: There is a high expansion and reliance on solar energy, which is proved by the presence of 161 green energy businesses.
- Transportation: 900 smart LED stop signs were installed; 400 buses became 4G vehicles; 120 buses were equipped with the technology to facilitate traffic management; almost 4,000 micropositioning smart devices were installed to provide users with instant information for food services.

- Water: Technology was applied in 11 important river channels and 4 hydropower stations to boost conservancy through 4G image monitoring.
- Education: Related services were improved by applying hotspots to create a "cloud tour" platform, connecting more than 500 000 teachers and students. Innovative teaching is triggered by "4G Portable Action Apps" used by more than 270 primary and secondary schools.
- Health Care: The Community Health Stations allowed the use of "Smart Health" 4G devices, enabling blood pressure and glucose test data integration for its use in hospitals and clinics.
- Tourism: The industry was boosted by applications that provide information on local merchants. As of 2020, the number of users has surpassed 4 million.
- Alliances: The collaboration between the academia, public sector, and private companies allowed linking AI with other technological solutions and its use in transportation and traffic systems, prevention systems, education, health care, tourism, or the environment.

Integrating the IoT for smart services is reshaping contemporary society and opening new opportunities for urban development, and as a consequence, increasing the comfort and well-being of the citizens in a knowledge society (Hsiao et al., 2021).

Education for Smart Cities and IoT

The world changes daily due to technology, generating the need for constant training. Various apps are released to generate various educational and business tasks; new models of computers and cell phones are put on the market every month and their functionalities increase, which has an impact on information management. When thinking about making smart cities a reality, it must be understood that a change must be generated in the education of new citizens and professionals for this process to be successful and sustainable.

Education for Smart Cities

One of the first components that should be part of education is multidiversity, that is, multicultural education (Aguaded-Ramírez, 2017; Liu et al., 2017) having specific cases like Thailand (Arphattananon, 2018). Culture is different even between citizens from different regions in the same country and, more clearly, with migrants from other countries who arrive for jobs, the vast majority (Monachesi, 2020). However, multicultural education also occurs among students in universities who develop classes with colleagues from other countries who do internships and can generate an amalgam of knowledge, friendship and, above all, understanding of another worldview, another perception of the world (Nageswara Rao et al., 2019; Raihani, 2018). One of the main characteristics of smart cities is that they collect the opinions and preferences of citizens to generate disruptive solutions to classic problems and propose a new form of management (Del-Aguila-Arcentales et al., 2020). One of the main characteristics of smart cities is that they collect the opinions and preferences of citizens to generate disruptive solutions to classic problems and propose a new form of management (Alvarez-Risco & Del-Aguila-Arcentales, 2021). In that sense, cities that take into account the opinion of their citizens, especially taking into account the opinion of part of the population that has grown up in other realities and under other cultural realities will make projects aimed at creating a sustainable city have a broader vision and can achieve the expected benefits.

Another fundamental content for the creation of the smart city is the environmental management of the city, which not only explains the care of natural resources but also implies the conversion of productive activities under the criterion of sustainability (Fortes et al., 2019; Varela-Candamio et al., 2018). The academic training of citizens in schools and, additionally, in universities is a cornerstone in the implementation of technology that allows detailed control of business activities in a country. In this scenario, it is vital that university education has a very strong data science component to be able to analyze large amounts of data and to generate predictive analytics that help build a smart city, regardless of the professional career you have. This must be a multidisciplinary development.

International business will accelerate as the smart city ensures great interaction between different countries and even other smart cities where the negotiation for international business is carried out based on the same smart structure of both cities.

Education for IoT

Smart education refers to an interactive and collaborative approach, which aims to enhance student creativity, engagement, and achievements (Malik & Shanwal, 2015). In an attempt to move from a teacher-centered to a student-centered approach, teachers need to adapt to learners' skills and learning preferences (Arseven et al., 2016; Keiler, 2018). It also involves the enhanced application of digital technologies (Mercader, 2020).

Smart education, which emphasizes modern knowledge, practical skills, and collaborative attitudes (Zhu et al., 2016) is an essential element in constructing a smart city (Jiang, 2020). Continuous investing in e-learning infrastructure, lifelong learning, R&D, and innovation in educational technologies are essential to produce smart graduates (Zhang et al., 2017). Young teachers who are digital natives are more prominent believers in the real impact of technology on education that aims to prepare students better to face the challenges of the future world (Deloitte, 2021). Young people require high technological literacy to live, study, and work effectively in the times of the Fourth Industrial Revolution (IDB, 2018).

Closing Remarks

The IoT will continue to change the lives of people and companies, invigorating businesses in an unexpected way, completely changing the conception of classic businesses and promoting various forms of advertising, payment, inventory management, and storage management. International businesses have been maintained in times of the COVID-19 pandemic and even when they are already recovering, it remains to be mentioned that technology is being installed more every day in the countries, facilitating coordination between companies, generating new sales, optimizing processes, allowing a detailed record and transforming society. There is a very big challenge for colleges and universities: educating for the development of a smart city. This implies that work must be done to develop the profile of the citizen of a smart city and implement in their basic, secondary, and university level training content that helps to create a smart city, both cultural elements that facilitate interculturality as well as development of technological competencies that help citizens to adapt to the technology that is increasingly changing and that is an essential part of smart cities. The challenge is launched and we hope that teachers and researchers will continue to generate and transmit new knowledge.

References

Aba, E. N., Olugboji, O. A., Nasir, A., Olutoye, M. A., & Adedipe, O. (2021). Petroleum Pipeline Monitoring Using an Internet of Things (IoT) Platform. *SN Applied Sciences, 3*(2), 180. https://doi.org/10.1007/s42452-021-04225-z

Accorsi, R., Bortolini, M., Baruffaldi, G., Pilati, F., & Ferrari, E. (2017). Internet-of-Things Paradigm in Food Supply Chains Control and Management. *Procedia Manufacturing, 11,* 889–895. https://doi.org/10.1016/j.promfg.2017.07.192

Aguaded-Ramírez, E. (2017). Smart City and Intercultural Education. *Procedia – Social and Behavioral Sciences, 237,* 326–333. https://doi.org/10.1016/j.sbspro.2017.02.010

Agyeman, J., & McLaren, D. (2017). Sharing Cities. *Environment: Science and Policy for Sustainable Development, 59*(3), 22–27. https://doi.org/10.1080/00139157.2017.1301168

Ahad, M. A., Paiva, S., Tripathi, G., & Feroz, N. (2020). Enabling Technologies and Sustainable Smart Cities. *Sustainable Cities and Society, 61,* 102301. https://doi.org/10.1016/j.scs.2020.102301

Alfian, G., Syafrudin, M., & Rhee, J. (2017). Real-Time Monitoring System Using Smartphone-Based Sensors and NoSQL Database for Perishable Supply Chain. *Sustainability, 9*(11). https://doi.org/10.3390/su9112073

Almeida, T. D., Costa Avalone, M., & Fettermann, D. C. (2020). Building Blocks for the Development of an IoT Business Model. *Journal of Strategy and Management, 13*(1), 15–32. https://doi.org/10.1108/JSMA-07-2019-0130

Alvarez-Risco, A., & Del-Aguila-Arcentales, S. (2021). Crowdsourcing for Sustainability: Case of Sustainable Development Goals. In R. Lenart-Gansiniec & J. Chen (Eds.), *Crowdfunding in the Public Sector: Theory and Best Practices* (pp. 187–196). Springer International Publishing. https://doi.org/10.1007/978-3-030-77841-5_12

Arphattananon, T. (2018). Multicultural Education in Thailand. *Intercultural Education, 29*(2), 149–162. https://doi.org/10.1080/14675986.2018.1430020

Arseven, Z., Sahin, S., & Kiliç, A. (2016). Teachers' Adoptation Level of Student Centered Education Approach. *Journal of Education and Practice, 7*(29), 133–144.

Barthélemy, J., Verstaevel, N., Forehead, H., & Perez, P. (2019). Edge-Computing Video Analytics for Real-Time Traffic Monitoring in a Smart City. *Sensors, 19*(9). https://doi.org/10.3390/s19092048

Ben-Daya, M., Hassini, E., & Bahroun, Z. (2019). Internet of Things and Supply Chain Management: A Literature Review. *International Journal of Production Research, 57*(15–16), 4719–4742. https://doi.org/10.1080/00207543.2017.1402140

Ben Letaifa, S. (2015). How to Strategize Smart Cities: Revealing the SMART Model. *Journal of Business Research, 68*(7), 1414–1419. https://doi.org/10.1016/j.jbusres.2015.01.024

Carr, M., & Lesniewska, F. (2020). Internet of Things, Cybersecurity and Governing Wicked Problems: Learning from Climate Change Governance. *International Relations, 34*(3), 391–412. https://doi.org/10.1177/0047117820948247

Chamola, V., Hassija, V., Gupta, V., & Guizani, M. (2020). A Comprehensive Review of the COVID-19 Pandemic and the Role of IoT, Drones, AI, Blockchain, and 5G in Managing its Impact. *IEEE Access, 8*, 90225–90265. https://doi.org/10.1109/ACCESS.2020.2992341

Chien, C.-F., Chen, H.-T., & Lin, C.-Y. (2020). A Low-Cost on-Street Parking Management System Based on Bluetooth Beacons. *Sensors, 20*(16). https://doi.org/10.3390/s20164559

City Keys. (2016). *Recommendations for a Smart City Index.* Retrieved 11/28/2021 from https://nws.eurocities.eu/MediaShell/media/CITYkeys%20D3.3%20-%20Recommendations%20for%20the%20Smart%20City%20Index.pdf

de Vass, T., Shee, H., & Miah, S. J. (2021). IoT in Supply Chain Management: A Narrative on Retail Sector Sustainability. *International Journal of Logistics Research and Applications, 24*(6), 605–624. https://doi.org/10.1080/13675567.2020.1787970

Dehgani, R., & Jafari Navimipour, N. (2019). The Impact of Information Technology and Communication Systems on the Agility of Supply Chain Management Systems. *Kybernetes, 48*(10), 2217–2236. https://doi.org/10.1108/K-10-2018-0532

Del-Aguila-Arcentales, S., Alvarez-Risco, A., & Rosen, M. A. (2020). Sustainable Cities. In A. Alvarez-Risco, M. Rosen, S. Del-Aguila-Arcentales, & D. Marinova (Eds.), *Building Sustainable Cities: Social, Economic and Environmental Factors* (pp. 51–63). Springer International Publishing. https://doi.org/10.1007/978-3-030-45533-0_5

Deloitte. (2021). *How to Build Value for Customers with the Internet of Things.* Retrieved 11/28/2021 from https://www2.deloitte.com/us/en/pages/chief-marketing-officer/articles/benefits-of-iot-to-consumers.html

Díaz-Díaz, R., Muñoz, L., & Pérez-González, D. (2017). Business Model Analysis of Public Services Operating in the Smart City Ecosystem: The Case of SmartSantander. *Future Generation Computer Systems, 76*, 198–214. https://doi.org/10.1016/j.future.2017.01.032

Ding, K., Jiang, P., & Su, S. (2018). RFID-Enabled Social Manufacturing System for Inter-enterprise Monitoring and Dispatching of Integrated Production and Transportation Tasks. *Robotics and Computer-Integrated Manufacturing, 49*, 120–133. https://doi.org/10.1016/j.rcim.2017.06.009

Falvo, M. C., Lamedica, R., Bartoni, R., & Maranzano, G. (2011). Energy Management in Metro-transit Systems: An Innovative Proposal Toward an Integrated and Sustainable Urban Mobility System Including Plug-in Electric Vehicles. *Electric Power Systems Research, 81*(12), 2127–2138. https://doi.org/10.1016/j.epsr.2011.08.004

Farahani, B., Firouzi, F., & Chakrabarty, K. (2020). Healthcare IoT. In F. Firouzi, K. Chakrabarty, & S. Nassif (Eds.), *Intelligent Internet of Things: From Device to Fog and Cloud* (pp. 515–545). Springer International Publishing. https://doi.org/10.1007/978-3-030-30367-9_11

Firouzi, F., Farahani, B., Weinberger, M., DePace, G., & Aliee, F. S. (2020). IoT Fundamentals: Definitions, Architectures, Challenges, and Promises. In F. Firouzi, K. Chakrabarty, & S. Nassif (Eds.), *Intelligent Internet of Things: From Device to Fog and Cloud* (pp. 3–50). Springer International Publishing. https://doi.org/10.1007/978-3-030-30367-9_1

Foreseeing Innovative New Digi Services. (2021). *About us.* Retrieved 11/28/2021 from https://www.find. org.tw/index/page/index/ABOUT_US

Fortes, S., Santoyo-Ramón, J. A., Palacios, D., Baena, E., Mora-García, R., Medina, M., Barco, R. (2019). The Campus as a Smart City: University of Málaga Environmental, Learning, and Research Approaches. *Sensors, 19*(6). https://doi.org/10.3390/s19061349

Furszyfer Del Rio, D. D., Sovacool, B. K., Bergman, N., & Makuch, K. E. (2020). Critically Reviewing Smart Home Technology Applications and Business Models in Europe. *Energy Policy, 144,* 111631. https://doi. org/10.1016/j.enpol.2020.111631

García-Berná, J. A., Ouhbi, S., Benmouna, B., García-Mateos, G., Fernández-Alemán, J. L., & Molina-Martínez, J. M. (2020). Systematic Mapping Study on Remote Sensing in Agriculture. *Applied Sciences, 10*(10). https://doi.org/10.3390/app10103456

Garg, S., Mittal, S. K., & Sharma, S. (2017). Role of E-trainings in Building Smart Cities. *Procedia Computer Science, 111,* 24–30. https://doi.org/10.1016/j.procs.2017.06.005

Ghauri, P., Strange, R., & Cooke, F. L. (2021). Research on International Business: The New Realities. *International Business Review, 30*(2), 101794. https://doi.org/10.1016/j.ibusrev.2021.101794

Gonçalves, F., Ferreira, J. C., & Campos, P. (2019). Improving the Tourists' Experience. Human Work Interaction Design. Designing Engaging Automation, Cham.

Haghi Kashani, M., Madanipour, M., Nikravan, M., Asghari, P., & Mahdipour, E. (2021). A Systematic Review of IoT in Healthcare: Applications, Techniques, and Trends. *Journal of Network and Computer Applications, 192,* 103164. https://doi.org/10.1016/j.jnca.2021.103164

Handscombe, J., & Yu, H. Q. (2019). Low-Cost and Data Anonymised City Traffic Flow Data Collection to Support Intelligent Traffic System. *Sensors, 19*(2). https://doi.org/10.3390/s19020347

Haque, M. M., Chin, H. C., & Debnath, A. K. (2013). Sustainable, Safe, Smart – Three Key Elements of Singapore's Evolving Transport Policies. *Transport Policy, 27,* 20–31. https://doi.org/10.1016/j. tranpol.2012.11.017

Harshitha, M., Rupa, C., Priya, B. B., Sowmya, K., & Sandeep, N. (2021). An Intelligent and Smart IoT-Based Food Contamination Monitoring System. Proceedings of International Conference on Computational Intelligence and Data Engineering, Singapore.

Hashem, I. A. T., Chang, V., Anuar, N. B., Adewole, K., Yaqoob, I., Gani, A., . . . Chiroma, H. (2016). The Role of Big Data in Smart City. *International Journal of Information Management, 36*(5), 748–758. https://doi.org/10.1016/j.ijinfomgt.2016.05.002

High-level Advisory Group on Sustainable Transport. (2016). *Mobilizing Sustainable Transport for Development.* Retrieved 11/28/2021 from https://sustainabledevelopment.un.org/index.php?page= view&type=400&nr=2375&menu=1515

Hsiao, Y. C., Wu, M. H., & Li, S. C. (2021). Elevated Performance of the Smart City – A Case Study of the IoT by Innovation Mode. *IEEE Transactions on Engineering Management, 68*(5), 1461–1475. https://doi.org/ 10.1109/TEM.2019.2908962

IBM. (2021). *How Industry 4.0 technologies are changing manufacturing.* Retrieved 11/28/2021 from https://www.ibm.com/topics/industry-4-0

IDB. (2018). *The Digital Transformation Imperative: An IDB Science and Business Innovation Agenda for the New Industrial Revolution.* Retrieved 11/28/2021 from https://publications.iadb.org/en/digital-transformation-imperative-idb-science-and-business-innovation-agenda-new-industrial

Intelligent Community Forum. (2021). *Intelligent Community Awards.* Retrieved 11/28/2021 from https://www.intelligentcommunity.org/awards

Jagtap, S., Duong, L., Trollman, H., Bader, F., Garcia-Garcia, G., Skouteris, G., . . . Rahimifard, S. (2021). Chapter 5 – IoT technologies in the food supply chain. In C. M. Galanakis (Ed.), *Food Technology Disruptions* (pp. 175–211). Academic Press. https://doi.org/10.1016/B978-0-12-821470-1.00009-4

Ji, M., Kim, J., Jeon, L., & Cho, Y. (2015, 1–3 July 2015). Analysis of Positioning Accuracy Corresponding to the Number of BLE Beacons in Indoor Positioning System. 2015 17th International Conference on Advanced Communication Technology (ICACT).

Jia, L., Wang, J., Liu, Q., & Yan, Q. (2021). Application Research of Artificial Intelligence Technology in Intelligent Agriculture. The 10th International Conference on Computer Engineering and Networks, Singapore.

Jiang, D. (2020). The Construction of Smart City Information System Based on the Internet of Things and Cloud Computing. *Computer Communications, 150*, 158–166. https://doi.org/10.1016/j.comcom.2019.10.035

Keiler, L. S. (2018). Teachers' Roles and Identities in Student-Centered Classrooms. *International Journal of STEM Education, 5*(1), 34. https://doi.org/10.1186/s40594-018-0131-6

Khan, I. H., Khan, M. I., & Khan, S. (2020). Challenges of IoT Implementation in Smart City Development. Smart Cities – Opportunities and Challenges, Singapore.

Lee, S. M., & Lee, D. (2021). Opportunities and Challenges for Contactless Healthcare Services in the Post-COVID-19 Era. *Technological Forecasting and Social Change, 167*, 120712. https://doi.org/10.1016/j.techfore.2021.120712

Li, H., & Parlikad, A. K. (2016). Social Internet of Industrial Things for Industrial and Manufacturing Assets**Acknowledgments to Financial Support of Cambridge Trust and China Scholarship Council. *IFAC-PapersOnLine, 49*(28), 208–213. https://doi.org/10.1016/j.ifacol.2016.11.036

Liu, D., Huang, R., & Wosinski, M. (2017). Multicultural Perspective on Smart Learning in Smart Cities. In D. Liu, R. Huang, & M. Wosinski (Eds.), *Smart Learning in Smart Cities* (pp. 217–232). Springer Singapore. https://doi.org/10.1007/978-981-10-4343-7_9

Lundan, S. M. (2018). From the Editor: Engaging International Business Scholars with Public Policy Issues. *Journal of International Business Policy, 1*(1), 1–11. https://doi.org/10.1057/s42214-018-0007-y

Maksimovic, M. (2018). Greening the Future: Green Internet of Things (G-IoT) as a Key Technological Enabler of Sustainable Development. In N. Dey, A. E. Hassanien, C. Bhatt, A. S. Ashour, & S. C. Satapathy (Eds.), *Internet of Things and Big Data Analytics Toward Next-Generation Intelligence* (pp. 283–313). Springer International Publishing. https://doi.org/10.1007/978-3-319-60435-0_12

Malik, N., & Shanwal, V. K. (2015). A Comparative Study of Academic Achievement of Traditional Classroom and Smart Classroom Technology in Relation to Intelligence. *Educational Quest, 6*(1), 21–24. http://fresno.ulima.edu.pe/ss_bd00102.nsf/RecursoReferido?OpenForm&id=PROQUEST-41716&url= https://www.proquest.com/scholarly-journals/comparative-study-academic-achievement/docview/1689386913/se-2?accountid=45277

McKinsey & Comapny. (2020). *How COVID-19 Has Pushed Companies over the Technology Tipping Point – And Transformed Business Forever*. Retrieved 11/28/2021 from https://www.mckinsey.com/business-functions/strategy-and-corporate-finance/our-insights/how-covid-19-has-pushed-companies-over-the-technology-tipping-point-and-transformed-business-forever

Meijer, A., & Bolívar, M. P. R. (2015). Governing the Smart City: A Review of the Literature on Smart Urban Governance. *International Review of Administrative Sciences, 82*(2), 392–408. https://doi.org/10.1177/0020852314564308

Mentzer, J. T., DeWitt, W., Keebler, J. S., Min, S., Nix, N. W., Smith, C. D., & Zacharia, Z. G. (2001). Defining Supply Chain Management [https://doi.org/10.1002/j.2158-1592.2001.tb00001.x]. *Journal of Business Logistics, 22*(2), 1–25.

Mercader, C. (2020). Explanatory Model of Barriers to Integration of Digital Technologies in Higher Education Institutions. *Education and Information Technologies, 25*(6), 5133–5147. https://doi.org/10.1007/s10639-020-10222-3

Min, S., Zacharia, Z. G., & Smith, C. D. (2019). Defining Supply Chain Management: In the Past, Present, and Future [https://doi.org/10.1111/jbl.12201]. *Journal of Business Logistics*, *40*(1), 44–55.

Monachesi, P. (2020). Shaping an Alternative Smart City Discourse through Twitter: Amsterdam and the Role of Creative Migrants. *Cities*, *100*, 102664. https://doi.org/10.1016/j.cities.2020.102664

Mostafa, N., Hamdy, W., & Alawady, H. (2019). Impacts of Internet of Things on Supply Chains: A Framework for Warehousing. *Social Sciences*, *8*(3). https://doi.org/10.3390/socsci8030084

Nageswara Rao, A. A., Warad, D. M., Weaver, A. L., Schleck, C. D., & Rodriguez, V. (2019). Cross-Cultural Medical Care Training and Education: A National Survey of Pediatric Hematology/Oncology Fellows-in-Training and Fellowship Program Directors. *Journal of Cancer Education*, *34*(3), 478–487. https://doi.org/10.1007/s13187-018-1326-8

Nicholls, L., Strengers, Y., & Sadowski, J. (2020). Social Impacts and Control in the Smart Home. *Nature Energy*, *5*(3), 180–182. https://doi.org/10.1038/s41560-020-0574-0

Parasuraman, A. (2000). Technology Readiness Index (Tri): A Multiple-Item Scale to Measure Readiness to Embrace New Technologies. *Journal of Service Research*, *2*(4), 307–320. https://doi.org/10.1177/109467050024001

Parry, G. C., Brax, S. A., Maull, R. S., & Ng, I. C. L. (2016). Operationalising IoT for Reverse Supply: the Development of Use-visibility Measures. *Supply Chain Management: An International Journal*, *21*(2), 228–244. https://doi.org/10.1108/SCM-10-2015-0386

Pérez-Pons, M. E., Plaza-Hernández, M., Alonso, R. S., Parra-Domínguez, J., & Prieto, J. (2021). Increasing Profitability and Monitoring Environmental Performance: A Case Study in the Agri-Food Industry through an Edge-IoT Platform. *Sustainability*, *13*(1). https://doi.org/10.3390/su13010283

Popova, I., Abdullina, E., Danilov, I., Marusin, A., Marusin, A., Ruchkina, I., & Shemyakin, A. (2021). Application of the RFID technology in logistics. *Transportation Research Procedia*, *57*, 452–462. https://doi.org/10.1016/j.trpro.2021.09.072

Raihani, R. (2018). Education for Multicultural Citizens in Indonesia: Policies and Practices. *Compare: A Journal of Comparative and International Education*, *48*(6), 992–1009. https://doi.org/10.1080/03057925.2017.1399250

Rainie, L., & Anderson, J. (2017). *The Internet of Things Connectivity Binge: What Are the Implications?* Retrieved 11/28/2021 from https://www.pewresearch.org/internet/2017/06/06/the-internet-of-things-connectivity-binge-what-are-the-implications

Rathore, M. M., Paul, A., Ahmad, A., Chilamkurti, N., Hong, W.-H., & Seo, H. (2018). Real-time Secure Communication for Smart City in High-speed Big Data Environment. *Future Generation Computer Systems*, *83*, 638–652. https://doi.org/10.1016/j.future.2017.08.006

Rosenbaum, M. S., & Wong, I. A. (2015). If You Install It, Will They Use It? Understanding Why Hospitality Customers Take "Technological Pauses" from Self-Service Technology. *Journal of Business Research*, *68*(9), 1862–1868. https://doi.org/10.1016/j.jbusres.2015.01.014

Roy, S. K., Balaji, M. S., Quazi, A., & Quaddus, M. (2018). Predictors of Customer Acceptance of and Resistance to Smart Technologies in the Retail Sector. *Journal of Retailing and Consumer Services*, *42*, 147–160. https://doi.org/10.1016/j.jretconser.2018.02.005

Saad, M. H., Hamdan, N. M., & Sarker, M. R. (2021). State of the Art of Urban Smart Vertical Farming Automation System: Advanced Topologies, Issues and Recommendations. *Electronics*, *10*(12). https://doi.org/10.3390/electronics10121422

Salem, M., Tsurusaki, N., Divigalpitiya, P., & Kenawy, E. (2020). An Effective Framework for Monitoring and Measuring the Progress towards Sustainable Development in the Peri-Urban Areas of the Greater Cairo Region, Egypt. *World*, *1*(1). https://doi.org/10.3390/world1010001

Schaffers, H., Komninos, N., Pallot, M., Trousse, B., Nilsson, M., & Oliveira, A. (2011). Smart Cities and the Future Internet: Towards Cooperation Frameworks for Open Innovation. The Future Internet, Berlin, Heidelberg.

Schmid, V., Doerner, K. F., & Laporte, G. (2013). Rich Routing Problems Arising in Supply Chain Management. *European Journal of Operational Research, 224*(3), 435–448. https://doi.org/10.1016/j.ejor.2012.08.014

Schwab, K. (2016). *The Fourth Industrial Revolution: What it Means, How to Respond*. Retrieved 11/28/2021 from https://www.weforum.org/agenda/2016/01/the-fourth-industrial-revolution-what-it-means-and-how-to-respond

Singh, R. P., Javaid, M., Haleem, A., & Suman, R. (2020). Internet of Things (IoT) Applications to Fight Against COVID-19 Pandemic. *Diabetes & Metabolic Syndrome: Clinical Research & Reviews, 14*(4), 521–524. https://doi.org/10.1016/j.dsx.2020.04.041

Smart city China. (2021). *Smart City China*. Retrieved 11/28/2021 from http://www.smartcitychina.cn

Stobierski, T. (2021). *International Business Examples to learn from*. Retrieved 11/23/2021 from https://online.hbs.edu/blog/post/international-business-examples

Strange, R., & Zucchella, A. (2017). Industry 4.0, Global Value Chains and International Business. *Multinational Business Review, 25*(3), 174–184. https://doi.org/10.1108/MBR-05-2017-0028

Tabaa, M., Monteiro, F., Bensag, H., & Dandache, A. (2020). Green Industrial Internet of Things from a smart Industry Perspectives. *Energy Reports, 6*, 430–446. https://doi.org/10.1016/j.egyr.2020.09.022

Timeus, K., Vinaixa, J., & Pardo-Bosch, F. (2020). Creating Business Models for Smart Cities: A Practical Framework. *Public Management Review, 22*(5), 726–745. https://doi.org/10.1080/14719037.2020.1718187

Turber, S., vom Brocke, J., Gassmann, O., & Fleisch, E. (2014). Designing Business Models in the Era of Internet of Things. Advancing the Impact of Design Science: Moving from Theory to Practice, 9th Design Science: Moving (2014). Designing business International Conference, DESRIST 2014, Miami, FL, USA, May 22–24, 2014. Proceedings 9 (pp. 17–31). Springer International Publishing, Cham.

United Nations. (2018). *68% of the World Population Projected to Live in Urban Areas by 2050, Says UN*. Retrieved 11/28/2021 from https://www.un.org/development/desa/en/news/population/2018-revision-of-world-urbanization-prospects.html

Varela-Candamio, L., Novo-Corti, I., & García-Álvarez, M. T. (2018). The Importance of Environmental Education in the Determinants of Green Behavior: A Meta-Analysis Approach. *Journal of Cleaner Production, 170*, 1565–1578. https://doi.org/10.1016/j.jclepro.2017.09.214

Vienna University of Technology. (2017). *European Smart Cities*. Retrieved 11/28/2021 from http://www.smart-cities.eu

Visvizi, A., Lytras, M. D., Damiani, E., & Mathkour, H. (2018). Policy Making for Smart Cities: Innovation and Social Inclusive Economic Growth for Sustainability. *Journal of Science and Technology Policy Management, 9*(2), 126–133. https://doi.org/10.1108/JSTPM-07-2018-079

Vlahogianni, E. I., Kepaptsoglou, K., Tsetsos, V., & Karlaftis, M. G. (2016). A Real-Time Parking Prediction System for Smart Cities. *Journal of Intelligent Transportation Systems, 20*(2), 192–204. https://doi.org/10.1080/15472450.2015.1037955

Walravens, N. (2012). Mobile Business and the Smart City: Developing a Business Model Framework to Include Public Design Parameters for Mobile City Services. *Journal of Theoretical and Applied Electronic Commerce Research, 7*(3). https://doi.org/10.4067/S0718-18762012000300011

Williamson, B. (2015). Educating the Smart City: Schooling Smart Citizens through Computational Urbanism. *Big Data & Society, 2*(2), 2053951715617783. https://doi.org/10.1177/2053951715617783

Wu, S. M., Chen, T.-c., Wu, Y. J., & Lytras, M. (2018). Smart Cities in Taiwan: A Perspective on Big Data Applications. *Sustainability, 10* (1). https://doi.org/10.3390/su10010106

Yu, X., & Zhang, B. (2019). Obtaining Advantages from Technology Revolution: A Patent Roadmap for Competition Analysis and Strategy Planning. *Technological Forecasting and Social Change, 145*, 273–283. https://doi.org/10.1016/j.techfore.2017.10.008

Zanella, A., Bui. N, Castellani, A., Vangelista, L., & Zorzi, M. (2014). Internet of Things for Smart Cities. *IEEE Internet of Things Journal, 1*(1), 22–32. https://doi.org/10.1109/JIOT.2014.2306328

Zhang, C., & Chen, Y. (2019). A Review of Research Relevant to the Emerging Industry Trends: Industry 4.0, IoT, Blockchain, and Business Analytics. *Journal of Industrial Integration and Management, 05*(01), 165–180. https://doi.org/10.1142/S2424862219500192

Zhang, Z., Cao, T., Shu, J., Zhi, M., Liu, H., & Li, Z. (2017, 27–29 June 2017). Exploration of Blended Teaching Pattern Based on Hstar and Smart Classroom. 2017 International Symposium on Educational Technology (ISET).

Zhu, Z.-T., Yu, M.-H., & Riezebos, P. (2016). A Research Framework of Smart Education. *Smart Learning Environments, 3*(1), 4. https://doi.org/10.1186/s40561-016-0026-2

Zong, S., Li, S., & Shang, Y. (2020). Optimal Quality-Based Recycling and Reselling Prices of Returned SEPs in IoT Environment. Intelligent Decision Technologies, Singapore.

Letitia Larry
Chapter 6
The Internet of Things (IoT) in Project Management

Introduction

Over the past two decades, project management has moved to the forefront as it relates to the tracking and management of epic shared service, cloud and Anything as a Service (XaaS) transformation efforts, as well as minor intra-enterprise modifications to practices, policies, solutions, and services. As digital transformation has become one of the most prevalent transition to transformation (T2T) experiences for public agencies and commercial firms, a look into the current state and associated maturity of the Internet of Things (IoT) as it relates to project management may assist with providing a basis for the future of major change efforts.

As the field of information technology (IT) has evolved as a discipline and tool, along with the technologies that support the discipline and enterprise, there have been corresponding changes to business, processes, practice, policy, services, and solutions. One area of change over the past five years has been in digital transformation, the expansion, movement, and/or sharing of intellectual property without human intervention, also referred to as the IoT (Van der Meulen, 2018). The more data there is the more data there is to secure and manage. This has called for an expansion of knowledge and expertise associated with data management and specifically the expansion of data security beyond current regulatory policy for personally identifiable information (PII). Government agencies, health care providers and insurers, financial institutions and other organizations collect large amounts of data on every transaction. The amount of data generated continues to grow at an exponential rate. Big data has a direct impact on IT staff that supports the effort (Stahl, 2012). New data and document control systems, software, and infrastructure to move, process, and store this information are being developed as older systems have become obsolete. IT staff are responsible for developing solutions to manage big data. With the advent or expanded acceleration of IoT, the responsibility of managing untouched (by human hands) data has moved to the forefront. Those who manage the portfolios, programs – and more specifically the projects utilizing nonhuman methods of transformation such at bots, are now responsible for resolving the issue of data security and management associated with the IoT.

https://doi.org/10.1515/9783110734133-006

Project Management

Project management consists of oversight of business and technical engagements, within and across enterprises, in support of successfully fulfilling mandated requirements (PMI.org, 2020). A project manager normally leads these types of efforts. Larger, interrelated, more complex projects are deemed programs. For larger projects, or programs, there may be several subprojects requiring a program manager who is responsible for the overall program and the associated project managers who are responsible for different work domains within the program. When there are several programs owned by a specific domain, then a portfolio of programs and projects exist.

The program or project manager is responsible for exercising the project management life cycle (PMLC) which consists of creation of a project management plan that details how the project or program will be executed and ensures that all involved parties are privy to overall status of the project or program and the associated responsibilities of each party/resource (i.e., technical staff, business and financial staff, contract/consulting staff, partners/vendors, stakeholders, customers, etc.) The Project Management Plan (PMP) includes subordinate plans including plans for stakeholder engagement, budget, schedule, scope, communications, requirements, resources, risk, change, test/verification, and quality. The compilation and concatenation of the information for the PMP an abundance of data and information with contributions across domains and resource types. The PMP not only contains an abundance of information, but it also produces a phenomenal amount of information that stipulates whether the program or project is on track, where there are failures or where there may be issues if not corrected. Information, data, is required for a project or program to be successful.

Information may be housed in a project management information system (PMIS). The PMIS may be a structure contained within a shared holder or a concatenation of several systems that house data related to different components of the portfolio, program, and/or project. The means of obtaining necessary information and data has changed since the infancy of defined and formalized project management in the 1990s.

Data Management

Data management as it relates to project management includes the creation, storage, and sharing of all necessary information, data points, that come from the initiation of a project, through the project management life cycle to project closure. Data management is defined as "the practice of collecting, keeping, and using data securely, efficiently, and cost-effectively" (Oracle, 2020, p. 1).

The goal of data management is to help people, organizations, and connected things optimize the use of data within the bounds of policy and regulation so that they can make decisions and take actions that maximize the benefit to the organization.

Managing digital data in an organization involves a broad range of tasks, policies, procedures, and practices. The work of data management has a wide scope, covering factors such as how to:

- Create, access, and update data across a diverse data tier
- Store data across multiple clouds and on premises
- Provide high availability and disaster recovery
- Use data in a growing variety of apps, analytics, and algorithms
- Ensure data privacy and security
- Archive and destroy data in accordance with retention schedules and compliance requirements (Oracle, 2020, p. 1)

There is an overwhelming amount of data that is fed into, created within and processed through the PMLC/PLC. There is data pulled from and created due to the initial business case and the associated business and technical requirements; data created to define, configure, and create the solution to be provided in response to the requests for the project or program (of projects); data created while configuring, developing, and migrating systems, solutions and data; and data output to prove, verify, and validate all components of delivery of the project solution. Every piece of information is data.

The data that flows from the project or program (of projects) must be managed. Data is managed manually or via tools as part of the PMIS. The PMIS is the intermediary between the data that flows to, within, through, and out of the project. The IoT is the cord that binds the massive amount of data that is produced.

IoT

"The Internet of Things is a system of interrelated computing devices, mechanical and digital machines, objects, or people that are provided with unique identifiers (UIDs) and the ability to transfer data over a network without requiring human-to-human (H2H) or human-to-computer (H2C) interaction," (Gillis 2016, p. 1). Today, devices and systems are an integral part of any project. The IoT has evolved and has expanded into many industries – including project management. Devices (desktops, laptops, tablets, mobile phones, smart devices, etc.) and systems (servers, databases, the cloud) are a component of most projects. Project managers use several, or multiple, devices to remain connected and to share information and data with project team members, customers, business partners/vendors, and other stakeholders. Gartner states that there are 20.4 billion connected devices (Gartner, 2019).

The IoT provides benefits for project managers, including but not limited to:

- Reduced or better managed workload as project managers have devices and repositories of information readily available requiring less, limited, or no manual intervention. Information may be pulled via query, reports, and other status indicators via large pools of data that is always available.

- Supported view of the current state of projects, programs, and the portfolio via shared services, XaaS or cloud-based PMIS project solution repositories.
- Accessible data that has already been collected and compiled and may be used for decision science. Information may be shared with customers, stakeholders, and other decision makers allowing for quick, accurate final determinations toward resolution of project concerns, risks, and issues.
- Support for program and project execution as current, relevant data is synchronized, systems are accessible by all involved in the program/project and collaboration is instilled in the project/program execution process.
- Expanded program director, program manager, and project manager roles as modifications to the size and complexity of projects has allowed for the expansion of project-related roles and a decrease in management from resources outside of the project team. Additionally, project managers include monitoring and management – and the associated escalation path – within the project or program role assignments thus allowing for timely resolution of any concern as there is direct access to necessary information/data.
  - Program directors own the overall success of the projects, program, and/or portfolio and serve as a member of any executive steering committee with the customer sponsor/executive.
  - Program managers function as integrators of IoT and the associated communications across domains and entities (i.e., enterprises and agencies).
  - Project managers are responsible for timely, successful execution of specific domains, and/or work products. For small projects, a project manager may be responsible for all tasks associated with those normally owned by a program manager or program director for large or complex programs and portfolios.
- Concentration on PMIS and other tool security to ensure project data is contained within the project and receptacle and only relevant project human resources, team members, have access and the ability to input, extract, and review contained data (raw data, information, reports, etc.) Role-based access to data is part of PMIS security practices.

The Importance and Benefits of IoT for Project Management

The IoT allows for the control of processes through automation, which in turn reduces costs associated with additional project human resources, project management and delivery, and offers project team, customer, and stakeholder transparency into project/program health and current state. Streamlined processes and the associated project data is accessible at anytime from anywhere, using sponsored smart devices with

secure applications, policy, practices, and standards in place. IoT also offers organizational benefits as follows:
- Monitoring of business processes associated with project management
- Improved project management and self-service experience
- Project and program time and cost savings
- Enhanced project team productivity
- Expansion, integration, and/or adaption of project and/or program business, technology, and delivery models
- More refined project/program decision science
- Increased revenue via expanded solutions and services offered during the PMLC

Advantages and Disadvantages of IoT for Project Management

There are advantages (mostly) and disadvantages of IoT within the project management discipline. One advantage is the ability to access data from the PMIS at any time using secure, approved devices. But this can also be a disadvantage as the ability to access data using a myriad of devices from anywhere using a secure connection may undermine the work/home life balance. Other advantages of IoT in project management are:
- Increased efficiency via big data. Big data makes information automatically measurable and analyzable.
- Improved communication(s). Stakeholders can directly access information/data on project health and status at any time without disturbing other team members.
- Dashboards, status reports and the associated raw data can be consumed by anyone having access at any time. If shared communications are clear, concise and correct, access to continuing and ongoing communications is an advantage.
- Data may be transferred over a connected network in an automated fashion. One secure pipeline, without human intervention, saves time and money.

The list of disadvantages of IoT in project management include: (a) a hacker may misappropriate confidential information; (b) the more devices there are the more data there is that requires management; (c) one corrupted device will most likely impact all connected devices; and (d) there may be compatibility/connectivity issues across devices manufactured by different companies and/or in different countries, as there are no international IoT standards.

Separate from the lists of advantages and disadvantages are impacts of IoT devices on project management. Impacts may be positive, negative or neutral in that the balance may go either way depending on the information and the personalities involved. IoT devices may affect project management in the following ways:
- Faster Reporting: Connected devices can generate and retrieve information in an automated fashion spawning sequential generation of data and reports making the project and its phases independent.

- Real-time Observation: Project phases and results may be observed in real time producing an overall view that may allow for movement of the project to an agile structure and methodology.
- On-Demand Data Bank: With IoT, used or generated project data can be made immediately available for use, which may be helpful for other similar projects.
- Data Trends: Data may create predictions and possible solutions to problems.
- Expectations: Due to ongoing data injection and availability, there are limited excuses for delays in project implementation, delivery and closure.

IoT Frameworks

A framework is a method, means, and technology to manage a specific resource. There are multiple frameworks used to manage IoT. The leading companies and the associated tools used for IoT follow in alphabetical order:
- Amazon Web Services (AWS) IoT is a cloud computing platform framework designed to enable smart devices to easily connect and securely interact with the AWS Cloud and other connected devices.
- Microsoft's Azure IoT Suite is a platform consisting of services that enable users to interact with and receive data from IoT devices, as well as perform operations over data, such as multidimensional analysis, transformation and aggregation, and visualize those operations.
- Google's Brillo/Weave is a platform for the rapid implementation of IoT applications consisting of two main backbones: Brillo, an android-based operating system (OS) for the development of embedded low-power devices; and Weave, an IoT-oriented communication protocol that serves as the communication language between the device and the cloud.
- Ericsson's Calvin is an open source IoT platform designed for building and managing distributed applications that enable devices to talk to each other that includes a development framework for application developers, as well as a runtime environment for handling the running application.

Trends and Future Prospects

The IoT is firmly rooted in the project management discipline and will remain so, per future trends as predicted by leading technology research and prediction firms (Forbes, Gartner) and technologists within leading technology firms (Amazon Web Services, Google, Microsoft, Oracle, etc.). Data continues to grow such that big data will remain one of the leading components of the IoT along with artificial intelligence (AI). AI is used to predict what systems and systems operators/technologists need and will do, as it relates to decision science via machine learning. Project management requires easily accessible, accurate information/data to (a) configure and develop systems; (b) make decisions on the way ahead for projects and programs; (c) predict concerns, risks, and issues prior to realization; and (d) take alternate, cost-effective routes to ensure successful verification, validation, and acceptance of systems and solutions. Project management, big data, and IoT are bound for any successful engagement.

Key Terms and Definitions

Big Data: Large volumes of data, both structured and unstructured, that inundates a business on a day-to-day basis; larger, more complex data sets, especially from new data sources (Gartner, 2019, pp. 2–3).

Bot: A software application that runs automated tasks (scripts) over the internet. Also known as crawler, internet robot, internet bot, robot, web robot, and spider (Angrishi 2017, p. 1).

Cloud Computing: A platform to provide on demand a shared pool of resources to end users across the globe using the internet. Such shared pools of resources are hosted on physical servers located in massive geodistributed data centers (DCs) (Chaudhary, Aujla, Kumar, & Rodrigues 2018, p. 2).

Data Management: The practice of collecting, keeping, and using data securely, efficiently, and cost-effectively (Oracle 2020, p. 1).

Internet of Things (IoT): A system of interrelated computing devices, mechanical and digital machines, objects, animals, or people that are provided with unique identifiers (UIDs) and the ability to transfer data over a network without requiring human-to-human or human-to-computer interaction (Gillis et al., 2016).

Project Management: The application of knowledge, skills, tools, and techniques to project activities to meet the project requirements (PMI.org, 2020).

Project Management Life Cycle also known as **project life cycle (PLC):** The series of phases that a project passes through from its start to its completion (i.e., initiation, planning, monitoring and controlling, executing and closing (PMI.org, 2020).

References

[2019] Internet of Things (IoT) Trends Barometer. (2020). *Gartner* online, January 8, 2020. https://www.gart ner.com/en/documents/3979284

Angrishi, K. (2017). Turning Internet of Things (IoT) into Internet of Vulnerabilities (IoV): IoT Botnets. Last modified February 12, 2017. https://arxiv.org/pdf/1702.03681.pdf

Chaudhary, R., Aujla, G. S., Kumar, N., & Rodrigues, J. J. P. C. (2018).Optimized Big Data Management across Multi-Cloud Data Centers: Software-Defined Network-Based Analysis. *IEEE Communications Magazine, 18*, 118–126. doi:10.1109/MCOM.2018.1700211

De Mauro, A., Greco, M., & Grimaldi, M. (2015). A Formal Definition of Big Data Based on its Essential Features. *Library Review, 65*(3), 122–135. doi.org/10.1108/LR-06-2015-0061

Gillis, A. S. (2016). What is the internet of things (IoT)? https://www.techtarget.com/iotagenda/definition/ Internet-of-Things-IoT, p1

IOT Agenda. (2020). TechTarget online. Accessed November 8, 2020. https://internetofthingsagenda.tech target.com/definition/Internet-of-Things-IoT

Jones, N. (2020). The Top 10 Emerging Trends and Technologies Driving the Future of IoT. Gartner. Webinar, 60 minutes. https://www.gartner.com/en/webinars/3894862/the-top-10-emerging-trends-and-technologies-driving-the-future-o

Longwood, J. (2019). Hype Cycle for Application Services. Last modified July 25, 2019. https://www.gartner. com/en/documents/3953608

Mavani, P. (2019). The Internet of Things and the Future of Project Management." Last modified January 16, 2019. https://cancanit.com/internet-of-things-and-the-future-of-project-management/

PMI Lexicon of Project Management Terms. (2020). PMI.org. Accessed November 29, 2020. https://www. pmi.org/pmbok-guide-standards/lexicon

Stahl, G. (2012). Big Data. Last modified August 19, 2012. https://eiuperspectives.economist.com/technol ogy-innovation/big-data-0

Towers-Clark, C. (2019). Big Data, IoT and AI, Part One: Three Sides of the Same Coin. Last modified, February 15, 2019. https://www.forbes.com/sites/charlestowersclark/2019/02/15/big-data-iot-and-ai-part-one-three-sides-of-the-same-coin/?sh=586e8e4269da

Van der Meulen, R. (2018). What Edge Computing for Infrastructure and Operations Leaders. Last modified October 3, 2018. https://www.gartner.com/smarterwithgartner/what-edge-computing-means-for-infrastructure-and-operations-leaders/

What Is Data Management? (2020). Accessed November 29, 2020. https://www.oracle.com/database/ what-is-data-management/

What Is Project Management? (2020). PMI.org. Accessed November 8, 2020. https://www.pmi.org/about/ learn-about-pmi/what-is-project-management

Soma Arora and Chaitanya Kohli
Chapter 7
The Rise of Surface Mobility in India

Introduction

During the course of evolution of mankind, wheels, and *Gothenburg Press* were arguably the most important inventions. There is sane logic to it. Wheels made mass travel
possible and *Gothenburg Press* made dissemination of information plausible. Eventual
advancements in science and technologies made travel and dissemination of information take place at a breakneck pace. Subsequently came the eureka moment of travel
for leisure as travellers got acquainted with the beauties and bounties on offer by
mother nature. Through Google and online travel agents (OTA) like MakeMyTrip, GoI-
bibo, Expedia, among others, a family living in a remote place could actually travel to
a breathtaking place like Hawaii within a few clicks.

E-Commerce in India

India was the world's fastest-growing GDP until COVID-19 happened. With ever-
increasing internet and mobile penetration across the board, e-commerce showed tremendous business growth in India (see Figure 7.1). Despite being the second-largest
user base in world, only behind China (650 million, 48% of population), the penetration of e-commerce was low compared to markets like the United States (266 million,
84%), or France (54 million, 81%), but is growing at an unprecedented rate, adding
around 6 million new entrants every month.

India's e-commerce market was worth about $3.9 billion in 2009, it went up to
$12.6 billion in 2013. In 2013, the e-retail segment was worth US$2.3 billion. About 70%
of India's e-commerce market was travel related. According to Google India, there
were 35 million online shoppers in India in 2014 Q1, expected to cross the 100 million
mark by the end of the year 2016. By 2020, India was expected to generate $100 billion
in online retail revenue out of which $35 billion was apparel sales set to grow four
times in coming years (Shettar, 2016).

With the advent of Jio (reliance data services) cheap mobile data had become
readily available across the length and breadth of the country. In fact, India had the
cheapest mobile data package rate in the whole world. This was accentuated and gal-
vanized into what is now termed as mobile commerce.

https://doi.org/10.1515/9783110734133-007

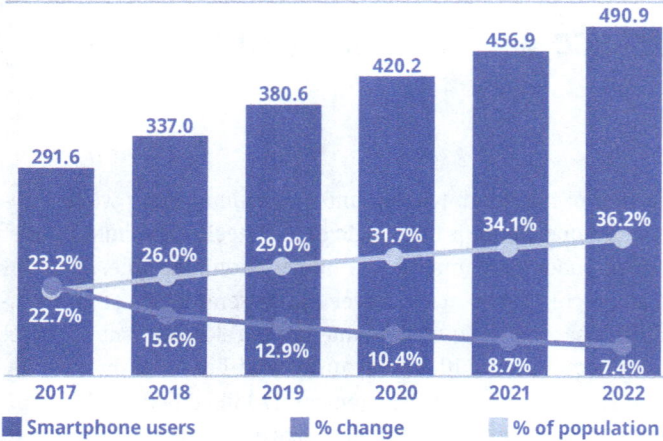

Figure 7.1: Smartphone users in India.
Source: *Forbes*, *Economic Times*, Inc42, Mobilityforesights.com,ecommerce-land

E-Business in India

We need milk, bread, and eggs every morning, which becomes a chore you may not enjoy a lot. Voila! There is an e-business that does exactly that named Milkbasket. As the fiscal year comes to a close, you start worrying about your tax filing. It pops up; Clear Tax. For every task, for everything you need, there is an e-business delivering value to you. Value to the customers is the cornerstone of most of these e-businesses.

The Surface Mobility Industry in India

Indian travel market (BCG & Google Travel Insights Report, 2017) was projected to grow by11.5% to the tune of $48 Billion by 2020. Aggregator platforms like GoIbibo, MakeMy-Trip, GoMMT, RedBus would certainly be piggybacking this growth trajectory accentuated by the fact that travel and tourism was one of those few industries which hardly ever go bust (barring the slump in pandemic times like COVID-19). Simultaneously, the internet penetration in the country was touching mind-boggling numbers due to ease of access and relatively pocket-friendly offerings. Since these companies relied heavily on easy access to internet services to bring customers onto the portal, the data clearly pointed toward the fact that there will be an ever-growing customer base for the company to serve to. If we now look closely at the actual industry that was served by travel portals, there was unprecedented growth: with higher disposable income, Indians were pouring more money into their travel to make it more comfortable including better hotels and other amenities.

Ever since giant advancements were made in the field of computing and related technologies, there emerged a plethora of aggregators making inroads into every segment closely associated with our daily lives. If it was groceries, click BigBasket, for needles to washing machines, click Amazon to book tickets, click Skyscanner, to book a hotel and for homestay, click Airbnb.

In the mobility segment, India – a country known for the lowest car ownership among all emerging countries – found a new answer to its mobility needs. The onslaught of various on-demand cab services viz. UBER, OLA, and other cab aggregators through API or application program interface (see Figure 7.2).

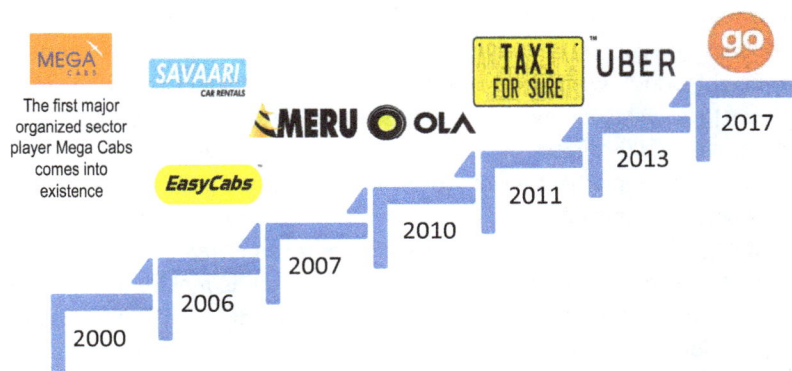

Figure 7.2: Growth of the organized taxi market in India.
Source: Karunakar (2016)

It was quite evident from the above timeline that GoCars from GoIbibo was a nascent player in the organized on-demand taxi market. Even though with great tech and a wide network of available cab partners, it was extremely difficult to penetrate the market and take a pie out of Uber or Ola market share, which is close to 90% in the segment. Having recently gone public, UBER's pocket was bigger than ever before (Karunakar, 2016).

The Business Model for Aggregators

In order to fully comprehend the modern business models in their robust digital frameworks one needed to understand the sources of value creation embedded in them. The sources of value addressed by the business model (Fuller & Morgan, 2011) construct can be addressed in three stages – 1. content, 2. structure, and 3. governance. At the *content* stage, the focus is on – information and goods being exchanged.

Resources and capabilities that are linked and goods, and financial capabilities required for exchanges are executed. In the second stage, that is, *structure,* the focus is on – network size; locus of control of construct that is being exchanged; ways in which parties exchange information, nature of control that enable exchanges; order and timing of mechanism. In the third stage – *governance,* the focus is on – trust, market mechanism, incentives, and flexibility (Bleier, Harmeling, & Palmatier, 2019).

This chapter is focused on the various aspects of the GoCars business model proposition, which lends serious insight into the development and success of the aggregator surface mobility business in India. MMT wanted to focus on a niche market strategy of differentiated offering. GoCars had its presence primarily in the following categories: rental cabs/outstation cabs/airport cabs. Even the modus operandi was different where it offered cabs not at the instant but for advance bookings with a minimum advance window of 2 hours. The authors have endeavored to map the process of improving GoCars' offering to its customers in the digital age. The study will provide valuable insight into how modern-day APIs were built to capture and deliver value to customers(Jayatilleke, Ranawakae, Wijesekera, & Kumarasinha, 2018).

The exercise is a two-fold process: B2B is a back-end activity where all the cab companies with single and multiple fleet owners provided the drivers and cabs while B2C at the front end where customers demand cabs as per their choice. The API (application programming interface) fetched the requirement and sent the order to the back end where the fleet was informed about the requirement and a cab is mobilized fulfilling that requirement. To understand the process of API development and effectiveness in business transformation we began at Stage 1, that is, content (Kuffer & Brecht, 2012).

Content Development: Product Management Team at Work

The product management team at any mobility app development unit goes through several stages (see Figure 7.3). In this chapter, the application of GoCars (front end B2C) and GoRyder (backend B2C),were the products. It was carefully crafted, focusing on user functionality and experience and moved ahead to roll out the product in the market and remove bottlenecks hampering its progress (Abramovici, 2007).

Step 1: Defining requirements: The process starts with the marketing team collaborating with engineers giving them the required logic and algorithms in their various coding languages to get the end system as to what we want our product to have and behave in the way we want.

Step 2: The marketing team worked as the optimizers, mastering the AB testing (2 versions of the User Interface is tested on an experimental basis).

Step 3: In the development phase, the Search Engine Optimization was mastered, and how to actually pursue the growth hacking in a limited budget and time frame. This

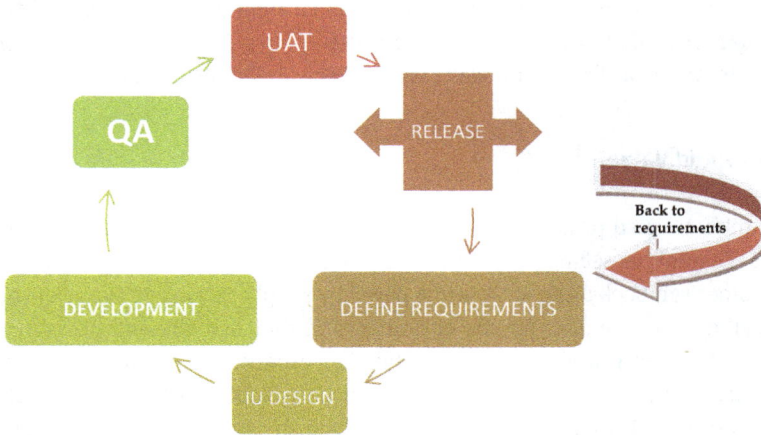

Figure 7.3: Stages in product management at application interface.
Source: Abramovici (2007)

also included campaigns designed in collaboration with the marketing team to increase the throughput and the actual revenue. An example was the IPL Go-Cash campaign where every time a user kept the app live while a match was going on, they would get Go-Cash in their wallet (Raphael & Zott, 2001).

Step 4: Question/Answer: Finally, the team worked in sync with the UX (user experience) designer to get the best look and feel of the product which will create utmost value and convenience for the prospective shopper on the app.

Step 5: UAT, user acceptance testing: As the name suggests it comes toward the end of the app development cycle. Once the app goes live, a very close eye was needed on app performance and issues if any faced by the shopper while creatively thinking of adding new features and tweaking certain processes, which could increase the throughput even further and enhance the long-term value for the customer while making them loyal customers.

Step 6: Release: The product is now ready to be released subject to suitable results delivered in UAT. If results are not favorable, the product goes for redefinition.

In this manner, the GoCars app was launched by GoIbibo (Wang & Fesenmaier, 2004). The team worked fervently on Google Analytics, search engine optimizer, and various related tools to enhance the visibility and subsequent conversion(reduce the bounce rate) of customers booking across platforms inclusive of both mobile apps and desktops.

Market research (including primary and secondary research) on the supplier side and also the front end, that is, the customer application for increasing efficiency and eking out bottlenecks while addressing the needs and issues. This included ground research along with providing a competitive business strategy to strongly establish and become a market leader in the niche cab category of airport mobility in the top five sectors of GoIbibo (Jayatilleke, Ranawaka, Wijesekera, & Kumarasinha, 2018).

Structure: How to Add Value?

GoIbibo offered differentiated products that included specialized airport cab pick-up and drop-off services. The unique selling proposition was while booking flight tickets through GoIbibo, the customer can book a cab at the same portal by simply clicking on the relevant tab. This cross-selling is convenient for the customer, and they actually end up saving some money owing to better prices offered for the bundled product. For example, booking a cab separately from anywhere in Bangalore to the airport costs Rs 820 while through flight funnel the cost is Rs 699 flat. In this manner, GoIbibo strives to convert features to benefits and further the value creation process (Remane, Hanelt, Nickerson, & Kolbe, 2017).

The Problem

While this seemed enticing enough, the bounce rate or the number of people entering the funnel and not ending up taking the taxi was upward of 95%. This is a classic conundrum that required a two-pronged approach, one of finding and eking out the bottle neck that was stopping the prospective client in moving to the next stage and the other to increase the actual size of the funnel itself (Bleier, Harmeling, & Palmatier, 2019).

The Research

The process started with Google Analytics wherein a customer journey funnel was created. Through this the authors were able to analyze the drop rates, which could be pinned on some part of the process (see Figure 7.4). (For better analysis, shoppers with less than 10 seconds of browsing time were removed, since people with such a short time span, might not be looking for something.)

Based on this (Xu, Shaoyi, Li, & Song, 2011) a research plan was devised using a two-pronged approach. First, to reduce the drops and subsequently increase the conversions while focusing on increasing the size of the funnel, that is, increasing visibility and hence the number of people landing on the page.

The Research Methodology

The research was exploratory in nature, trying to explore the consumer behavior involving – reasons they visited the site, the user experience, price offering expectations, comparison with competition, etc.

Closed Funnel Analysis
Filtered by segment: Users with greater than 10sec session time

Users completed   Users not completed   Users flow

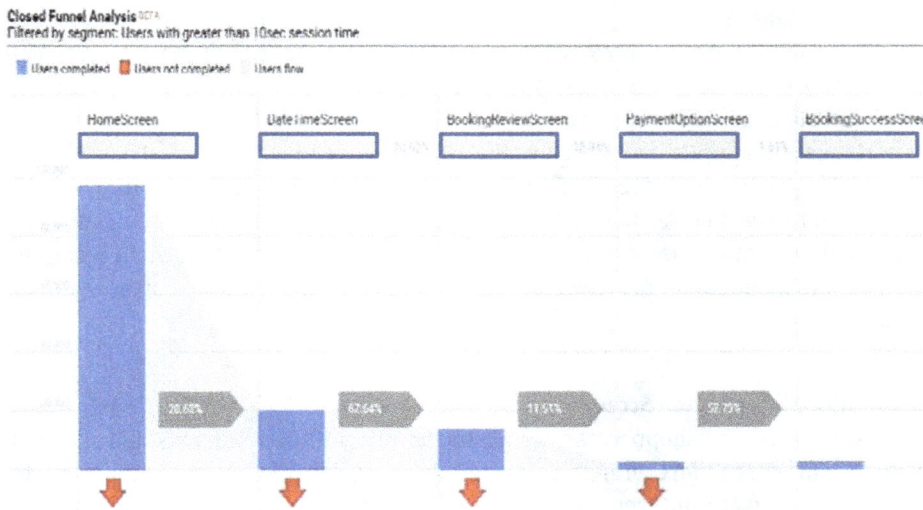

Figure 7.4: Google Analytics' view of the GoMMT website.

Further, there was a telephonic interview that was conducted separately for customers only on the home page and customers who advanced further in the booking process but did not finally book the cab.

Stratified random sampling was used during the process where each stratum was one of the major cities served by GoCars (Xiao, Wei, & Dong, 2016; Zhang et al., 2016).

Table 7.1: Analysis and findings of survey.

Issues	Percentage
High price	18%
Can't apply full Go-Cash	5%
Previous bad experience	5%
Difficulty in applying voucher	5%
Payment issues	14%
Trust issue	5%
Toggling without issues	36%
Worry of cancellation policy	9%
Instant cab	5%

Findings

Most of the findings pertaining to GOMMT indicated high Bounce rate and poor traffic management on the website. So there would be significant drop outs on the Home screen or failed transactions which have been highlighted in this section of the chapter. Going further, GOMMT took steps to mitigate these problems related to online presence.

Drop after Home Screen

Based on findings of the survey (see Table 7.1). Toggling was 36% of the reason constituting drop after visiting the home screen. There were multiple reasons for this drop. Some people come to home page to toggle and have a look. They were there just to experience the app. Others weren't able to figure out how to move ahead (This is where the product manager has his work cut out so that each transition step is smooth and easy even for non-tech savvy people). Still, others realized a cab offering from GoIbibo, which they could use subsequently as required. All of them made the majority who came in at the first stage and left creating the highest drop at the earliest stage.

Drop before Transaction Screen

At this juncture, the shopper had fed in all the relevant travel details and was at a state to compare cab fare with other portals like a regular user. Now it becomes tricky because, there were different vendors for different routes. This made some sectors cheaper than others as compared to the competitor enticing the customer enough to move to the next stage. But the comparison especially when the rates weren't favourable dropped the conversion rates drastically.

Failed Transaction

Another issue that popped up during the analysis was failed payment. While the industry standard for failed payments was around 5%, GoCar was clocking a failure rate of 8.30%, which translated to losing assured customers. What was even more concerning was that if this issue persisted from multiple transactions of a single user, they could forever abstain from the portal.

Approach to Rectification

Since it was decided to increase the size of the funnel as well as increase the conversion rate, the following was initiated (Pauwels & Weiss, 2008).

SEO Approach: In order to increase actual customers landing at the page and being made aware of GoIbibo cab offering, use Search Engine Optimization. The SEO process started by tracking various keywords and their respective search volumes using the tool Getstat. Next the corresponding keyword is in-depth analyzed for figuring out total clicks, conversion rate, average CTR and average position using Google Search Console.

Then through Google Analytics, the search rates of these key words were mapped. The average CTR (see Figure 7.5) was as low as 2.8%. This meant low engagement on the website. We also use past travel data on Redash, to figure routes where we are

Figure 7.5: Google Analytics' view of the GoMMT website.
Source: GoMMT.com

doing well and routes that are dilapidated and not being searched much. We finally garnered a list of 20 keywords each, both for airport routes and outstation routes, which have to be fully focused in order to increase the base and penetration.

Steps taken to increase the average search engine result page rankings:
- Creating links(URL) if not existent for that route.
- Making pages relevant through better recommendation logics for nearby routes and popular routes.
- Better meta linking of pages.
- Improving the overall summary of the page making it more relevant. All of this helped in increasing the search for all the keywords.

Once this activity was completed along with better targeting on search engine marketing (SEM), greater visibility of GoCars on google was ordained, whenever prospective shoppers came searching for cabs. This targeting resulted in more shoppers on the D-web and M-web and higher information that helps increase shoppers on the app itself (Günzel & Wilker, 2012).

Meta Search Approach: This was a specific type of search engine that gave results based on a variety of database from search engines. It specialized in concatenating databases from a variety of search engines and linking search results to relevant sources (see Figure 7.6). In this case, some well-known meta searches were prevalent, which got high volume of users on their portal. These portals like Sky Scanner, Trivago, Trip advisor, among others, compared rates and other amenities providing access to millions of flights and hotel rooms. A very relevant and focused strategy was pivotal for a company like GoMMT to showcase its range of offerings to customers who come to these portals.

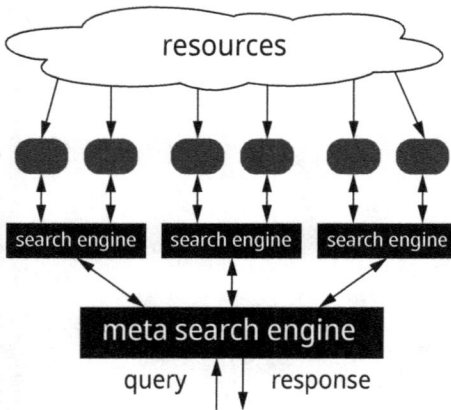

Figure 7.6: Search engine basics.
Source: Wikipedia

In our case, we worked to fine tune our meta search logic to include cab pick-up and drop-off for all the hotel and flight bookings. We increased the visibility of our cab offering along with flights on these portals to entice the customers with our convenient bundled offering.

Building Efficiency: Through Conversion Enhancement

Based on the findings above, some changes to the application were planned.
- There would be a change in the cancellation policy where customers who have booked cabs at the GoCar portal, wanting to cancel 12 hours before the journey wouldn't have to pay anything.
- There would be a completely new offering on the airport route for instant cab booking and boarding, pretty much like the competition.
- With greater access to vendors in very busy routes, a company can naturally bring down rates. Offering flat rates to any place in the city works wonders for a customer living a long way away from the airport and helps in saving them huge costs making them a loyal customers of the portal.
- There is a meeting planned with the payment team to eke out pertinent payment issues hampering some part of the revenue. This is true for both payments through UPI as well as Pay Pal, which is still in nascent stages in India.

Greater focus and putting the onus of wrongdoing in cases of bad experience for a customer, which is never to be repeated. Drivers below the 3.85 rating will not get future rides sending a strong signal across the board (Fuller & Morgan, 2011).

Introduction to MegaCab Integration Process at GoMMT

There has been enhanced focus by GoCars to cater to the niche airport so it can provide differentiated value to its customers. The company is already cross selling a bundled product by offering cabs to people booking a flight on the GoIbibo portal. This makes an overall convenient experience for the customer and through this process GoIbibo is trying to become a one-stop shop horizontally coalescing each product on a single shared customer journey. Now in order to go hack further, we were able to get mega cabs on board as one of our airports vendors. This came on the backdrop of a tremendous opportunity to tap into an instant booking game just like our competitors Uber and Ola. For implementing into in our systems, we had to redesign some aspects of our app and change the boarding process for the customer (Moon & Kamakura, 2017).

The New Transaction Structure

The new vendor implies that the way a customer boards their cab changes drastically. Earlier, the cabs were pre-booked, and the driver would meet the customer at the arrival bay with the customer already knowing all the details pertaining to their journey. This however, changes now. In either case – advanced or instant booking, the customer simply receives a QR code along with directions and instructions of simply walking to the Mega Cab airport kiosk to get their cab. This also brings in a lot of changes that need to happen at the back end when Mega Cab is on boarded as one of our airports vendors. The major change was felt on the modus operandi, too. The user cannot only book advance cabs for the airport journey, they can now also book a cab instantaneously once they land at the airport. This is particularly convenient in the Indian context since the on-time performance of Indian carriers is abysmally low at 74% (DGCA monthly air performance report March, 2019) meaning there's a 26% chance the flight is delayed and the customer with an advanced booking may end up paying late charges or even cancellation charges. (Only in case of flight funnel booking, do we track flight details giving real-time data to the cab driver who adjusts the pick-up time accordingly.)

Since there is a major change of approach of how a customer will now board the cab, the changes have to be reflected in the app itself and before that, all teams have to be on the same page of how the actual process would transpire. The following is the service blueprint of the process (see Figure 7.7).

Based on back-end data of the GoMMT app, the authors came out with a customer journey map as to how the process would work in transition. Afterwards, when the flow was finalized, a technical document was to be made which was called product requirement document (PRD) which details all the processes and changes that needs

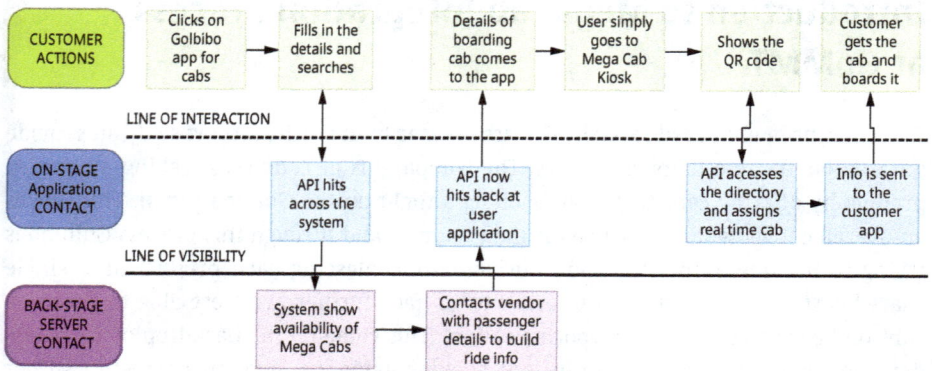

Figure 7.7: Process mapping of front and back end of the GoMMT app.
Source: GoIbibo web traffic data

to be made in the application and final look and feel of the app once the initiation has been done. PRD can be done on Helix ALM software or even simpler Google Sheets. What's important is that since multiple stakeholders are involved like designers, developers, coders, business development, and even the management, it's pivotal that the document is detailed enough and is vividly clear as to what are each team's expectations and what exactly they are supposed to do. Following is the designer's wireframe which helps to tell the actual look in the app itself, developed in consultation with the designer on the software called Zeplin.

The new set-up is now named "Book & Board."

The Way Forward

In conclusion, the authors would like to reiterate the importance of – novelty; lock-in; efficiency, and complementarities in securing value for the business model (see Figure 7.8).

As in the given model, it was seen that new transaction structures; new content; new participants were the source of novelty to the business. The inclusion of MEGA Cabs into the business adds a fresh lease on life.

There is efficiency of delivery through speed, scale economies, and simplicity by revamping the mobility app (Salomo, Steinhoff, & Trommsdorff, 2003).

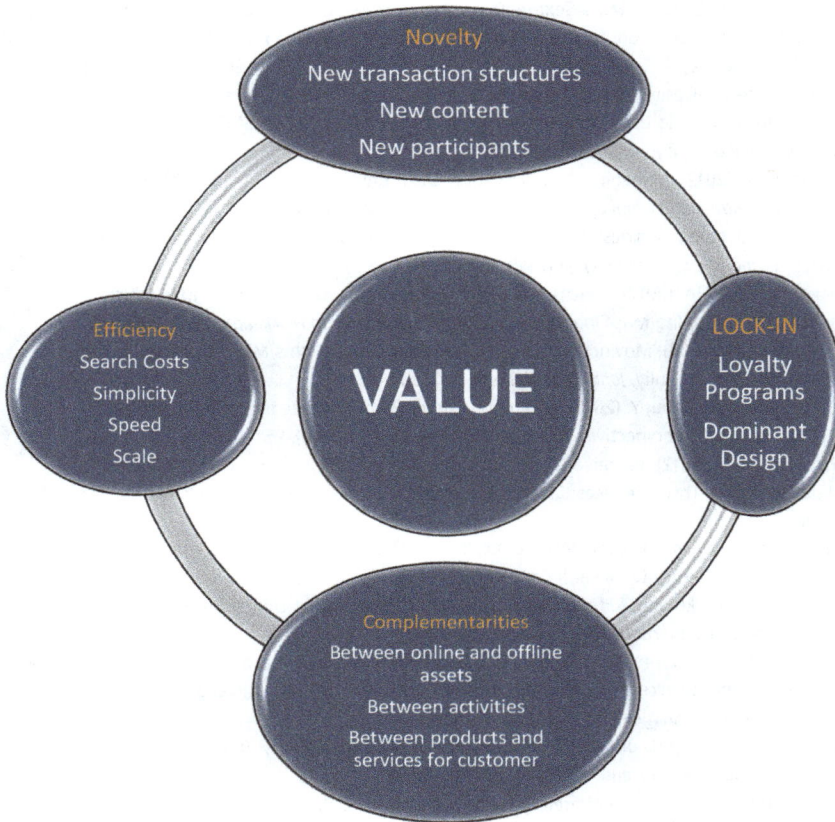

Figure 7.8: Creating value in the longrun.
Source: Pradeep Nilord (2012)

References

Abramovici, M. (2007). Future Trends in Product Lifecycle Management (PLM). In *The Future of Product Development*(pp. 665–674).Berlin, Heidelberg: Springer.

Amit, R., & Zott, C. (2001). Value Creation in E-business. *Strategic Management Journal, 22* (6–7), 493–520. Applications, 11 (6).

Baden-Fuller, C., & Morgan, M. S. (2010). Business Models as Models. *Long Range Planning, 43*(2–3), 156–171.

BCG, Google (2017). Demystifying the Indian Online Traveller. Retrieved from: https://media-publications. bcg.com/BCG-Google-Demystifying-the-Indian-online-traveler-Jun-2017.pdf

Bleier, A, Harmeling, C. M., & Palmatier, R. W. (2019). Creating Effective Online Customer Experiences. *Journal of Marketing, 83*(2), 98–119.

Günzel, F., & Wilker, H. (2012). Beyond High Tech: The Pivotal Role of Technology in Start-up Business Model Design. *International Journal of Entrepreneurship and Small Business, 9, 15*(1), 3–22.

Hitt, M. A., Ireland, R. D., Camp, S. M., & Sexton, D. L. (2001). Strategic Entrepreneurship: Entrepreneurial Strategies for Wealth Creation. *Strategic Management Journal, 22*(6–7), 479–491.

Jayatilleke, B. G., Ranawaka, G. R., Wijesekera, C., & Kumarasinha, M. C. (2018). Development of Mobile Application Through Design-Based Research. *Asian Association of Open Universities Journal.*

Karunakar, B. (2016). Changing Paradigms in the Taxi Industry in India. *ACADEMICIA: An International Multidisciplinary Research Journal, 6*(5), 93–133.

Kuffer, F., & Brecht, L. (2012). Managing Product Variety Decisions for Sustainable Profitability in B2B Industries. *International Journal of Technology Marketing, 7*(3), 287–305.

MacInnes, I. (2005). Dynamic Business Model Framework for Emerging Technologies. *International Journal of Services Technology and Management, 6*(1), 3–19.

Moon, S., & Kamakura, W. A. (2017). A Picture Is Worth a Thousand Words: Translating Product Reviews into a Product Positioning Map. *International Journal of Research in Marketing, 34*(1), 265–285.

Pauwels, K., & Weiss, A. (2008). Moving from Free to Fee: How Online Firms Market to Change their Business Model Successfully. *Journal of Marketing, 72*(3), 14–31.

Qi, J., Zhang, Z., Jeon, S., & Zhou, Y. (2016). Mining Customer Requirements from Online Reviews: A product improvement perspective. *Information & Management, 53*(8), 951–963.

Racherla, P., & Friske, W. (2012). Perceived 'Usefulness' of Online Consumer Reviews: An Exploratory Investigation Across Three Services Categories. *Electronic Commerce Research and Applications, 11*(6), 548–559.

Raphael & Zott (2001). *Strategic Management Journal*, Special Issue: Strategic Entrepreneurship: Entrepreneurial Strategies for Wealth Creation. *22* (6–7), 479–491.

Remane, G., Hanelt, A., Nickerson, R. C., & Kolbe, L. M. (2017). Discovering Digital Business Models in Traditional Industries. *Journal of Business Strategy, 38*(2).

Salomo, S., Steinhoff, F., & Trommsdorff, V. (2003). Customer Orientation in Innovation Projects and New Product Development Success—The Moderating Effect of Product Innovativeness. *International Journal of Technology Management, 26*(5–6), 442–463.

Shettar. (2016). Emerging Trends of E-Commerce in India: An Empirical Study. *International Journal of Business and Management Invention, 5*(9), Dharwad, 25–31.

Wang, Y., & Fesenmaier, D. R. (2004). Modeling Participation in an Online Travel Community. *Journal of Travel Research, 42*(3), 261–270.

Xiao, S., Wei, C. P., & Dong, M. (2016). Crowd Intelligence: Analyzing Online Product Reviews for Preference Measurement. *Information & Management, 53*(2), 169–182.

Xu, K., Liao, S. S., Li, J., & Song, Y. (2011). Mining Comparative Opinions from Customer Reviews for Competitive Intelligence. *Decision Support Systems, 50*(4), 743–754.

Guido Rojer Jr.
Chapter 8
Digital Marketing and Globalization: The Opportunity for Caribbean Small Island Developing States

Introduction

Small Island Developing States (SIDS) have been identified to be vulnerable to external shocks due to their size, remoteness, and isolation (Briguglio, 1995). Combined, these limitations discourage the development of higher-order novelty, which are critical means to trade, learn, and specialize (Mohan, Watson, & Strobl, 2018). As a consequence, SIDS remains dependent on developments in foreign markets and acquires adaptive capabilities to respond to changing environments. Access to the global market is thus greatly determined by how island agents can adapt to established avenues and pathways to reach global markets. A seismic shift is taking place as technological platforms have transformed to allow for inexpensive universal access to markets all over the world. Inexpensive platforms such as Apple Music, Youtube, Facebook, Instagram, Fivver, OnlyFans, and TikTok allow islanders the opportunity to directly access markets abroad. Island agents now dispose of more control of their endeavors to partake in the process of globalization.

This approach is surely merited in allowing ease of access at relatively reduced costs, however, brings their own set of challenges for island brands. Since islands are isolated, island agents often customize their offerings to the tastes and preferences of the domestic market, akin to employing economies of scope as a strategy to penetrate the market. Such specialization may be difficult to scale in markets where brands are yet unknown (Lawton & Harrington, 2007). Caribbean SIDS have historically been rich in culture and creativity, which is increasingly becoming the foundation for the main source of value, and cause of the transaction. Like many nations in the Global South, these assets make up the local economy, which is rapidly growing, and require more attention to realize the value it may represent in global markets. This is a novel challenge for island agents, since, in addition to engaging in new technology for marketing, they may have to adapt to new markets elsewhere in the world.

Creative transactions have often been guided by editorial models, however, find their way to the market through (new) digital platforms that can engage isolated nodes into the global network. Island based firms (IBF) can benefit from adopting strategies to study and anticipate trends, in order to apply entrepreneurial bricolage in this foreign venture. Digital marketing is a specific aspect that requires further attention since this venture takes a local economy directly to the global level and may serve as vital for this transformation.

https://doi.org/10.1515/9783110734133-008

This chapter is structured as follows: Section 2 reviews the literature relevant to SIDS, isolation, and technological gaps, while also discusses technological trends that make up the 21st century. Section 3 provides an analysis of the strategies that can be employed utilizing these trends and developments in the context of SIDS, whereas Section 4 reviews avenues for future research, and draws to a close with contributions in Section 5.

Digital Marketing

Digital marketing (DM) has become an integral part of the marketing mix employed by small and medium-sized enterprises (SMEs), as digital platforms and technology has facilitated inexpensive and more direct access to customers (Gibson, 2018). Novel platforms and channels allow for both a broad reach with potential consumers, as well as a more personal connection with consumers. SMEs may see considerable improvement of business outcome when adopting DM as a strategic way to elicit the desired action by consumers, otherwise known as the conversion. With the development of these channels becoming more accessible over the course of time, SME strategies to convert leads have taken a variety of approaches (Bala & Deepak Verma, 2018). First it is also important to understand motives behind engagement with businesses, and then determining how these motives are brought into action on digital platforms. It should also be no surprise that companies need to know which channels are used by consumers, in order to achieve higher conversion through better targeting. Gibson (2018) identified DM strategies to include social media marketing, email marketing, search engine optimization, search engine marketing, digital public relations, online advertising, customer relationship management systems, content marketing, affiliate marketing, newsletters, and display marketing.

A review by Pradhan, Nigam, & Tiwari (2018) identified the need to studying how the opportunities created by digital marketing for Indian SMEs. These new strategic avenues have colored the modern marketing environment and prompts SMEs to rethink their market strategies. A subsequent review gave more direction as to how these gaps could be filled, by identifying four categories that make up this phenomenon: channels, social media, digital relationships, and digital technologies (Herhausen, Miočević, Morgan, & Kleijnen, 2020). They further define the challenges faced by SMEs in two gaps, one where managers current DM practices and ideal DM capabilities, and a second where DM transformations the yet have to match the actual body of knowledge that supports it. These two gaps determine how SMEs adopt DM and are able to realize business outcome improvement. According to Chatterjee & Kumar Kar (2020) it is perceived usefulness, perceived ease of use and compatibility that ultimately determines the choice between DM strategies.

Though it might seem that the definition of DM is universal, substantial differences in strategic application exist between geographical areas, as Matosas-López (2021) finds "European organizations confer great importance to the interaction with its audience, while American organizations tolerate a greater degree of one-way communication." A study by García, Lizcano, Ramos and Matos (2019), for example, found that voice searches from mobile devices could power the future lead generation activities, and would require substantial learning capabilities to adopt. Another study in the hospitality industry linked DM strategies and tactics like email marketing and to the volume and valence of online reviews and, indirectly, hotel performance (De Pelsmacker, van Tilburg, & Holthof, 2018).

Tiago and Verissimo (2014) found that managers need not immediately adopt the most advanced strategies but should focus on relationship-based interactions with their customers. Thus, with the variety of SMEs, managers should derive their own DM strategies to forge relationships with their customers depending on the situational needs. Social media marketing, for example, has been identified as a critical factor in influencing emotions and attachment to festival brands that create positive word of mouth as one of the desired outcomes (Hudson, Roth, Madden, & Hudson, 2015). This development underscores how involved customers have become in service provisions as customers seek agency solutions when they can no longer create on their own (Hughes & Vafeas, 2019). As such relationships are now at the core of DM because they provide insight and networks that concern sustainability and growth of business models (Saura, Palos-Sanchez, & Herráez, 2020). Another study found evidence in support of this claim, citing substantial benefits from relationship building when marketing services particularly through utilizing social media (Purcărea & Purcărea, 2017). Firms thus need to engage with customers in ways that enable connection and brand association that facilitates loyalty and return, which has the potential to truly realize the promise of an inexpensive tool.

These tools, though not completely universal, may position firms and their brands at a global level, which further underscores the inexpensive character of employing DM. Traditional markets examined in the studies cited are typically in larger countries, that can enable firm growth without substantial alterations to accommodate, for example, differences in culture that international firms face. As such the calls for geographical diversity deem it necessary to explore how areas where internationalization is an additional challenge.

Analysis

The size of the domestic market has been a key determinant in the strategic orientation of firms. For IBF it entails engaging in economies of scope, rather than economies of scale, as vulnerabilities and isolation create idiosyncrasies that frame how opportunities are perceived. First islands have elevated involvement of public administration which determines in great part how domestic market challenges emerge (Chittoo, 2011). Secondly, island governments are unable to stimulate their private sectors appropriately, since the tools are not designed to serve their reality (Minto-Coy, Lashley, & Storey, 2018). Furthermore Baldacchino (2020) argues that: "Island development trajectories are heavily impacted by their relevance, similarity, complementarity and value in relation to continental development pathways." In his chapter he discusses fundamental differences for islands that are near their former colonizer or mainland, versus those that are remote, and concludes that distance matters in how islands create opportunities. Remote islands are often more removed and respond better to the needs of their economies, from a political angle.

As such IBF operate in a highly politicized domestic environment where the development strategy attempts to employ tactics that are successful elsewhere, without achieving the corresponding results. Evidence indicates that Caribbean countries, develop at "a substantially lower level of income than other countries and that the intensive margin plays a greater role in this process" (Mohan, 2016). These gaps that currently discourage businesses and enable a departure the isolation that is currently limiting the islands' economies to expand. This implies that they face additional challenges when targeting foreign markets, and resort to strategic flexibility to maintain their position domestically (Baldacchino & Bertram, 2009).

It is remarkable to ascertain how international markets have increasingly become accessible to firms from all spaces, by making distance irrelevant in the process of targeting customers from abroad. This development specifically opens up new opportunities for IBF which face elevated challenges when considering expansion beyond domestic borders (Baldacchino & Fairbairn, 2006). For IBF this is yet another fundamental exogenous factor that requires adaptation to develop new competitive niches, that comes along with new orientations for growth (Baldacchino, 2019). Previously seen as out of reach IBF can now, with substantially more ease, organize to target, and convert, customers from abroad especially for rendering services utilizing DM strategies. A previous study of IBF in the Pacific that examined how managerial thinking and action influences the development of technology and marketing capabilities (Stern, Singh, & Dutt Pathak, 2014). The authors found support for the capability-performance that indicated it is action that creates the desired performance of DM, which renders the results. IBF would thus have to rely on effectuation to conceptualize this creation of new markets as it has become a more transformational process, rather than the traditional notion of search and select (Dew, Read, Sarasvathy, & Wiltbank, 2011). The opportunities offered by the digital space are increasingly creative, which account for the process becoming more transformational, and allows for the reimagination of offerings as well as the approach with regard to how DM activities convert customers (Ruyter, Isobel Keeling, & Ngo, 2018). The revolutions that DM are poised to make may require a more practical approach.

The activity of DM is becoming increasingly varied, and may entice IBFs to create presence and content in as many channels as possible, but would not contribute to the true potential of DM: which is targeting new markets in efficient ways. Since the true market growth potential of DM for IBF is in foreign markets, it is important to observe how firms already engaged in international markets engage with their customers. MNEs have been found to employ bricolage strategies to develop international opportunities (Yang, 2018), and provides an insight as to how IBF may also realize the opportunities of DM. These strategies involve co-innovation, and accelerating customer value, which can be facilitate through DM.

Bricolage is characterized by improvisation, which is the fundamental dynamic that promotes IE (Brown, Mawson, Rowe, & Mason, 2018). Firms assemble loose teams to experiment with relatively simple approaches to create favorable conditions for their products or services. Skills pertaining to this activity have been signalled to be transferrable, as a method that enables companies without these capabilities to acquire them (Sarasvathy & Venkataraman, 2011). Although foundations for DM, like information and data processing, automation of advertising technology, and the application of computers have contributed to firms (McGuigan, 2019), they have accelerated in the way they contribute to firms. Blazevic, Lievens, and Klein (2003) have identified these developments early on, especially considering the rise of mobile services, and their long term impact for firms. As these developments continue to evolve through network effects and connect customers to firms, IBF should resort to more application of effectuation and bricolage than before. Social and digital marketing offers significant opportunities to organizations through lower costs, improved brand awareness and increased sales. (Dwivedi et al., 2020) The lack of innovative technological strategies threatens digital-media corporations' ability to maintain marketplace sustainability for addressing disruptive innovation technologies like video co-creation (Acevedo-Berry, 2020). These activities allow engagement with potential customers and ultimately causes conversion, when utilizing DM tools.

This study takes the example from the creative industries, which have been successfully able to leverage their brand beyond borders. Musicians from the Caribbean have emerged as new sources of novelty in their industry, since the departure of the use of the editorial model. Musicians establish themselves through channels such as YouTube, Spotify, Instagram, Facebook, Apple Music independently and create a new stream of income, which scales their musical productions across markets. As such, an industry that would have otherwise been isolated connects itself to the global market by employing DM (Lourens et al., 2020). Musicians have been known to apply bricolage in their strategies, as they also leverage their brand name in collaboration with wider known national brands, or even firms with regional presence, through DM. Partnering for ads, curated music productions and jingles, brand ambassadorship, and co creations have, among others, allowed artists to create new revenue streams from their brand name built as musicians. These activities follow by utilizing other DM strategies such as TikTok challenges or hashtag campaigns that further popularize artists.

The Caribbean market itself has been very responsive in welcoming musicians from other islands that allowed musicians to further focus on their craft in an expanded market. Artists like Machel Montano from Trinidad & Tobago has become relatively popular in non soca territories like the Dutch Caribbean, whereas Aruba's Jeon has been able to leverage previous productions in hits with Colombia's JBalvin and Brazil's ANITTA. Curaçao's MENASA also achieved major success in licensing his production as sample to Bollywood film, becoming a major TikTok sensation and challenge in India and across the Diaspora. These examples may seem anecdotal but refer to the start of a trend where musicians have broken through on behalf of creatives to venture abroad through DM. The creative sector encompasses TV and movie production as well as radio and podcasts. Architects, (web) designers may also render services digitally and are prime candidates to develop and utilize DM capabilities.

IBF may face issues in choosing the right mix due to lack of capabilities and familiarity with use and application in foreign markets. This is a classic environment to apply bricolage theory, as it is a new situation to which agents apply existing knowledge.

Future Research Avenues

In the quest to optimize DM Tools firms need to organize in a way that corresponds with the most effective target audience channels available, in order to practice DM activities that elicit conversion. IBF are in the quest to develop foreign markets and need to employ DM tools and activities that are also different from those applied in home markets. As such IBF emerge as the true natural experiment to explore the impact of DM, as they offer a variety of benefits to increase economies of scale, as well as penetrate markets. These strategies are also welcomed given their inexpensive character, which enables more return for businesses operating at the scale of small islands.

When explaining DM strategies for IBF through the lens of bricolage, it is necessary to recognize that IBF operates in an environment where they have yet to develop tools to conquer foreign markets, much like entrepreneurs offering novelty in existing markets. As such bricolage theory is very suitable as it recognizes that capabilities are developed concurrently with actions, through the entrepreneurial process. Bricolage refers to actions and outcomes resulting from combining available resources to new problems (Fisher, 2012). In the case of IBF, resources and capabilities are yet to be developed to attain foreign markets, above all because of isolation. DM tools are additionally not employed in the same way, when targeting local audiences; because of the benefit home markets have to try out/experience branding physically.

As such it is necessary to have wider investigation as to how IBF may employ DM to grow abroad. It is necessary to study which markets would likely respond better, in order to determine which channels to employ when crafting a DM strategy. Concurrently this avenue ties into which industries would be the early adopters of DM strategies following the creatives. This could be telling as it may reveal whether disposition of local DM capabilities is a predictor of successful DM deployment when targeting foreign markets. Additionally, the field is calling to study the choice of DM strategies and the depth of usage to identify how these convert customers, and to append these efforts to the revenue they create in order to determine ROI.

It is also advisable to study how capabilities are developed as firms roll out DM strategies.

Contribution

This chapter highlights important aspects pertaining to DM for IBF. It acknowledges that globalization presents a unique opportunity for IBF, through DM. This is especially the case for the Caribbean region that boasts sizeable and substantial resources, which are fundamental for economic transactions and creating value. These opportunities represent inclusive, equitable and sustainable growth trajectories and requires attention from scholars, practitioners, and policymakers alike. DM, as well as skills, tools, and ecosystem, pertaining to this activity, is crucial to enable the globalization of IBF engaged in the creative economy. IBF should be strategic in DM activities and respond aggressively to those spaces that show initial interest by engaging with consumers. It is imperative to experiment with different strategies of DM, particularly discovering new target audiences through DM, as well as engaging with them to build brands utilizing these inexpensive tools. It is vital to understand marketing aspects that have been proven in these markets to avoid any mishaps that can tarnish efforts to build brands and relationships with these new audiences. It is clear that this opportunity requires considerably low effort, when contrasted with the potential outcomes that can be beneficial to IBF. The adoption of new platforms, or positioning in new markets may be extra sensitive to creative products or services that are linked to specific backgrounds that shape these markets. This process is theoretically explained through entrepreneurial bricolage, by which firms employ existing strategies to acquire DM capabilities. Additionally, the process of building brands may require IBF to relinquish aspects that have become successful in the domestic market for more responsive ones in new markets.

The main takeaway of this chapter lies in its response to calls for geographical diversity, which have shown critical departures from conventional thoughts about DM. In this case it introduces an international characteristic, where firms are presented with unique opportunities that would have not emerged without the Digital Revolution. As such these findings also encourage SMEs from other spaces to engage with markets and audiences abroad, through DM strategies.

References

Acevedo-Berry, L. M. (2020). *Successful Strategies to Address Disruptive Innovation Technologies in the Digital-media Industry.* Retrieved from https://scholarworks.waldenu.edu/dissertations

Bala, M., & Deepak Verma, M. (2018). A Critical Review of Digital Marketing Paper Type:-Review and Viewpoint. *International Journal of Management, 8*(10), 321–339.

Baldacchino, G. (2019). The Competitiveness of Small States: Insights on Flexible Specialisation. *Small States & Territories, 2*(1), 41–54. https://doi.org/10.1017/CBO9781107415324.004

Baldacchino, G. (2020). How Far Can One Go? How Distance Matters in Island Development. *Island Studies Journal, 15*(1), 25–42. https://doi.org/10.24043/isj.70

Baldacchino, G., & Bertram, G. (2009). The Beak of the Finch: Insights into the Economic Development of Small Economies. *Round Table, 98*(401), 141–160. https://doi.org/10.1080/00358530902757867

Baldacchino, G., & Fairbairn, T. I. J. (2006). Editorial: Entrepreneurship and Small Business Development in Small Islands. *Journal of Small Business and Entrepreneurship, 19*(4), 331–340. https://doi.org/10.1080/08276331.2006.10593374

Blazevic, V., Lievens, A., & Klein, E. (2003). Antecedents of Project Learning and Time-to-Market During New Mobile Service Development. *International Journal of Service Industry Management, 14*(1), 120–147. https://doi.org/10.1108/09564230310466010

Briguglio, L. (1995). Small Island Developing States and their Economic Vulnerabilities. *World Development.* https://doi.org/10.1016/0305-750X(95)00065-K

Brown, R., Mawson, S., Rowe, A., & Mason, C. (2018). Working the Crowd: Improvisational Entrepreneurship and Equity Crowdfunding in Nascent Entrepreneurial Ventures. *International Small Business Journal: Researching Entrepreneurship, 36*(2), 169–193. https://doi.org/10.1177/0266242617729743

Chatterjee, S., & Kumar Kar, A. (2020). Why Do Small and Medium Enterprises Use Social Media Marketing and What Is the Impact: Empirical Insights from India. *International Journal of Information Management, 53*, 102103. https://doi.org/10.1016/j.ijinfomgt.2020.102103

Chittoo, H. B. (2011). Public Administration in "Small and Island Developing States": A Debate about Implications of Smallness. *Global Journal of Management and Business Research, 11*(9), 23–34. Retrieved from https://globaljournals.org/GJMBR_Volume11/5-Public-Administration-in-small-and-strategic.pdf

De Pelsmacker, P., van Tilburg, S., & Holthof, C. (2018). Digital Marketing Strategies, Online Reviews and Hotel Performance. *International Journal of Hospitality Management, 72* (July 2017), 47–55. https://doi.org/10.1016/j.ijhm.2018.01.003

Dew, N., Read, S., Sarasvathy, S. D., & Wiltbank, R. (2011). On the Entrepreneurial Genesis of New Markets: Effectual Transformations Versus Causal Search and Selection. *Journal of Evolutionary Economics, 21*(2), 231–253. https://doi.org/10.1007/s00191-010-0185-1

Dwivedi, Y. K., Ismagilova, E., Hughes, D. L., Carlson, J., Filieri, R., Jacobson, J., . . . Wang, Y. (2020). Setting the Future of Digital and Social Media Marketing Research: Perspectives and Research Propositions. *International Journal of Information Management*, (May), 102168. https://doi.org/10.1016/j.ijinfomgt.2020.102168

Fisher, G. (2012). Effectuation, Causation, and Bricolage: A Behavioral Comparison of Emerging Theories in Entrepreneurship Research. https://doi.org/10.1111/j.1540-6520.2012.00537.x

García, J. J. L., Lizcano, D., Ramos, C. M. Q., & Matos, N. (2019). Digital Marketing Actions that Achieve a Better Attraction and Loyalty of Users: An Analytical Study. *Future Internet, 11*(6), 1–16. https://doi.org/10.3390/fi11060130

Gibson, C. (2018). The Most Effective Digital Marketing Strategies & Approaches: A Review of Literature. *International Journal of Scientific and Research Publications, 8*(2), 12. Retrieved from www.ijsrp.org

Herhausen, D., Miočević, D., Morgan, R. E., & Kleijnen, M. H. P. (2020). The Digital Marketing Capabilities Gap. *Industrial Marketing Management, 90*(August), 276–290. https://doi.org/10.1016/j.indmarman.2020.07.022

Hudson, S., Roth, M. S., Madden, T. J., & Hudson, R. (2015). The Effects of Social Media on Emotions, Brand Relationship Quality, and Word of Mouth: An Empirical Study of Music Festival Attendees. *Tourism Management, 47*, 68–76. https://doi.org/10.1016/J.TOURMAN.2014.09.001

Hughes, T., & Vafeas, M. (2019). Marketing Agency/Client Service-For-Service Provision in an Age of Digital Transformation. *Journal of Business-to-Business Marketing, 26*(3–4), 265–280. https://doi.org/10.1080/1051712X.2019.1611080

Lawton, T. C., & Harrington, D. G. (2007). Banking on Global Success: Internationalization Strategy and Its Limitations (The Case of Allied Irish Banks). *Thunderbird International Business Review, 49*(5), 630–631. https://doi.org/10.1002/tie

Lourens, J., Rojer, G., & Heyden, M. (2020). Like and Share. Social Media and Musicians in Small Island Developing States: The Case of Curaçao. *Academy of Management Global Proceedings, Mexico* (2020),214. https://doi.org/10.5465/amgblproc.mexico.2020.0214.abs

Matosas-López, L. (2021). The Management of Digital Marketing Strategies in Social Network Services: A Comparison between American and European Organizations. *Journal of Open Innovation: Technology, Market, and Complexity, 7*(1), 65. https://doi.org/10.3390/joitmc7010065

McGuigan, L. (2019). Automating the Audience Commodity: The Unacknowledged Ancestry of Programmatic Advertising. *New Media & Society, 21*(11–12), 2366–2385. https://doi.org/10.1177/1461444819846449

Minto-Coy, I. D., Lashley, J. G., & Storey, D. J. (2018). Enterprise and Entrepreneurship in the Caribbean Region: Introduction to the Special Issue. *Entrepreneurship and Regional Development, 30*(9–10), 921–941. https://doi.org/10.1080/08985626.2018.1515823

Mohan, P. (2016). Caribbean Diversification and Development. *World Economy, 39*(9), 1434–1453. https://doi.org/10.1111/twec.12387

Mohan, P., Watson, P., & Strobl, E. (2018). Nascent Entrepreneurs in Caribbean Small Island Developing States: Opportunity Versus Necessity. *Journal of Developmental Entrepreneurship, 23*(4), 1850022. https://doi.org/10.1142/S108494671850022X

Pacheco, B., & Pacheco, M. (2020). Digital Business Service Transformation of Caribbean Economies: A Path to Sustainability. *Small States & Territories, 3*(2), 413–432.

Pradhan, M. P., Nigam, D., & Tiwari, C. K. (2018). Digital Marketing & SMEs: An Identification of Research Gap via Archives of Past Research. *International Journal of Applied Engineering Research, 13*(8), 6089–6097. Retrieved from http://www.ripublication.com

Purcărea, T., & Purcărea, A. (2017). Services Marketing in the Era of Disruption and Digital Transformation. *Romanian Economic and Business Review, 12*(4), 7–26. Retrieved from http://www.rebe.rau.ro/RePEc/rau/journl/WI17/REBE-WI17-A1.pdf

Ruyter, K. de, Isobel Keeling, D., & Ngo, L. V. (2018). When Nothing Is What it Seems: A Digital Marketing Research Agenda. *Australasian Marketing Journal, 26*(3), 199–202. https://doi.org/10.1016/j.ausmj.2018.07.003

Sarasvathy, S. D., & Venkataraman, S. (2011). Entrepreneurship as Method: Open Questions for an Entrepreneurial Future. *Entrepreneurship: Theory and Practice, 35*(1), 113–135. https://doi.org/10.1111/j.1540-6520.2010.00425.x

Saura, J. R., Palos-Sanchez, P., & Herráez, B. R. (2020). Digital Marketing for Sustainable Growth: Business Models and Online Campaigns Using Sustainable Strategies. *Sustainability (Switzerland), 12*(3), 3–7. https://doi.org/10.3390/su12031003

Stern, N., Singh, G., & Dutt Pathak, R. (2014). Technology and Marketing Capabilities in a Developing Economic Context: Assessing the Resource-Based View within a Boundary Condition. *International Journal of Business and Economics*, *13*(1), 75–92.

Tiago, M. T. P. M. B., & Veríssimo, J. M. C. (2014). Digital Marketing and Social Media: Why Bother? *Business Horizons*, *57*(6), 703–708. https://doi.org/10.1016/j.bushor.2014.07.002

Yang, M. (2018). International Entrepreneurial Marketing Strategies of MNCs: Bricolage as Practiced by Marketing Managers. *International Business Review*, *27*(5), 1045–1056. https://doi.org/10.1016/j.ibusrev.2018.03.004

Aditya Kumar Gupta, Ashutosh Pillai, and Neelash Thallam

Chapter 9
Japanese Anime: Redefining Digital Story Telling

This chapter explores the journey of anime from its inception to how it defines story-telling in the digital world. It starts by giving a basic introduction to anime and the different types of genres. In subsequent sections, Kyoto Animation, also known as KyoAni, a major animation studio in Japan, is looked at to see how they managed to climb the ladder of success. KyoAni has proved to be a valuable subject to understand how a small studio from Japan managed to become one of the most successful studios in the world despite facing many difficulties.

The Origins of Anime

Gen Z and millennials' affection for anime has inspired filmmakers and companies to engage consumers with their movies and brands. Crunchyroll (Summer, Manga, anime) streaming service has reported 120 millions registered users. Anime has shown enhanced demand in the age demographic of 16 to 34 year-olds. Numerous brands have launched product lines inspired by anime. The Loew's studios Ghibil collection, Gucci's Doremon capsule collection, Sand Liang, and Vans apparel and sneaker collection, Color popx Sailor Moon Makeup Collection, Taco Bell's Manga style ad and comic book tie-in, etc. have successfully attracted Gen Z and the millennials.

In India, retail brand Celio launched menswear with Naruto, a popular anime, Pokemon and Attack on the Titan. In 2022, the anime market reached US\$ 25.62 billion, value wise, and is predicted to be doubled by 2032. Anime has shown rapid growth during the pandemic; market value is said to be set to enhance from US\$ 16.60 billion (2017–21) to US\$ 25.62 billion in 2022–32. This has increased consumer spending on online shows, popularity of media shows and increased anime production house profits. The quality and content of Japanese comic books and upgraded computer animation methods has enhanced anime acceptance among consumers globally. The following pages describe the anime journey.

The Anime Journey

Anime (pronounced ah-nee-may) is hand-drawn computerized animation having its origin in Japan. There are more than 7,000 anime. Anime in Japan means any sort of

https://doi.org/10.1515/9783110734133-009

animation regardless of its style and origin but for the rest of the world it simply means animated works from Japan. The earliest animated work dates back to 1917 and slowly started spreading and gaining attention. It is distributed theatrically, through television broadcasts, and over the internet (Netflix, Crunchyroll, Funimation, etc.).

Anime and its production are a very diverse medium with many distinct production methods and technologies. Graphic art, characterization, cinematography, and other sorts of inventive and individualistic skills are all combined in this process. A lot of such anime are adaptations of manga (Japanese comics). *Naruto* is a famous anime that was released on October 3, 2002, while the original manga was published first on September 21, 1999. The Naruto manga was the fourth highest selling manga series of all time and the entire Naruto franchise has made more than $10 billion to date.

A more recent example would be *Jujutsu Kaisen,* which had its first episode released on October 3, 2020, while the manga was published on July 4, 2018. The anime earned roughly around $133 million. There are many more anime and manga that have made more than this and have been more successful, not to mention the anime industry consists of more than 500 production studios, including major studios like Toei Animation, Kyoto Animation, Studio Ghibli, etc. This advancing technology has redefined animated content and has continued to increase its market share every year. The global anime market is expected to reach US$ 48.03 billion by 2028.

Figure 9.1: Available record of first anime.
Source: Anime, https://en.wikipedia.org/wiki/Anime#/media/File:Anime_cell_1917.jpg

History

Anime dates to the birth of the Japanese film industry (early 1900s) and has ended up becoming one of the major cultural forces over the past years (Figure 9.1). The early techniques did not include the use of sophisticated technologies and methods, they were simply hand drawn on film, paper cutouts, blackboards, etc.

After World War II, TOEI, one of the first modern Japanese animation production companies came into being. The animations they worked on and planned to release were inspired by Walt Disney Pictures as they were as popular in Japan as everywhere else. One key example of an anime of that time would be Akira Kurosawa's *Rashomon,* which brought attention to Japan's movie and entertainment industry. The major push the anime industry received was after the release of Mitsuteru Yokoma's *Sally the Witch, Kid with His Giant Robot* and *Tetsujin 28-go* which were adapted for TV by TOEI.

By the 1960s anime began showing up in English speaking areas as well. One of the first major animated exports to the United States was *Astro Boy,* adapted from Osamu Tezuka's *Manga* about a robot boy with superpowers. More anime was brought to the United States by purchasing rights and animations, and then promoting them. Peter Fernandez, Carl Macek, and Sandy Frank are a few of the important people who helped in spreading the Japanese anime culture. The viewers of these shows realized the hard work that had been done to tailor a smooth experience for the nonanime users, by re-dubbing in English, and removing scenes that would not be acceptable to the censor networks. Later audiences started demanding the original work be portrayed as a matter of principle. In a similar way more shows started showing up in different areas and parts of the world.

By the 1980s there was an increase in the number of anime studios, some of them managed to become successful while a few of them were not able to keep up with the competition. Anime continued to become more popular with even more breathtaking and detailed animations as technology improved and it became easier for illustrators and animators to compile things together.

Genres

Anime is classified over many genres and demographics. Komodo for children, Shoujo for young girls, Shonen for young boys, and a diverse range of genres targeting the adult audience. Shoujo and Shonen anime encompass an enormous variety of genres and styles that feature a variety of stories, emotions, and characters. What unites these genres is that they basically visualize and show the desires and wishes of their users, which increases the commitment of viewers to their shows. Genres like Seinen and Mecha target the audience that is more into sci-fi, robots, etc. There is a slice of life that has story lines revolving around real life situations, problems, and emotions like depression, hardship, love, reality, etc. Last but not least there are genres like Harem, Ecchi, and Isekkai that revolve more around sexual and flirty concepts. These types of genres are generally rated 16 or 17+ and rarely contain any sort of scenes that might need to be reviewed by the censor board. However, these are not to be confused with the genre that focuses on adults and is rated 18 or 20+; this genre is called Hentai. These genres are a subset of the adult industry and feature pornographic content. There are also genres that explore male and female homosexuality and are called Yaoi and Yuri, respectively. These types of anime have pornographic content but also content that focuses on relationship development and LGBT education.

The Japanese anime industry has a diverse range of genres that have further subsets. The industry focuses on its viewers and readers and wishes to give them what they need (Figure 9.2). This is one of the ways Japanese anime and the manga industry have such a huge following and market share.

Globalization

In the last 50 years, there has been a worldwide expansion in the production and distribution of anime media and products from Japan. It has sparked the growth of an equally strong global fan base, which is at the heart of anime's cultural phenomenon and commercial success. Although there are negative perceptions associated with anime, such as it being a trivial or juvenile activity, this misperception fails to account for the global popularity of anime and its fan base. Anime has effectively become a transcultural force as many countries, particularly the United States, have adopted it into their own popular cultures.

Emerging technology and the followers of the anime community, who actively share content across physical and digital mediums, are responsible for most of its international success. However, studies have revealed that anime is a globally distributed product by design, as it was created with the goal of being culturally odorless, or *mukokuseki* (Figure 9.3). One example is anime characters, who may be recognized as Japanese but are supposed to be phenotypically indistinguishable regarding race or ethnicity. This contributes to the adaptation of anime to the geographical, national, and cultural identities of the target audience. Anime is a one-of-a-kind depiction and vehicle of globalization, with a deceptively subtle strategy to integrate itself into other countries' popular culture consciousness. It is a unique gear in the wider media industrial machine, showcasing anime producers and the entertainment industry's collective societal responsibility to their fans.

Company Study

About

Kyoto Animation Co., Ltd., founded in 1940, with their headquarters in Uji, Kyoto prefecture, Japan, was chosen to analyze the increasing trend in Japanese anime. Kyoto Animation has published many top grossing and award-winning shows throughout the years, like *Clannad* (2007), *Violet Evergarden* (2018), *Miss Kobayashi's Dragon Maid* (2017),

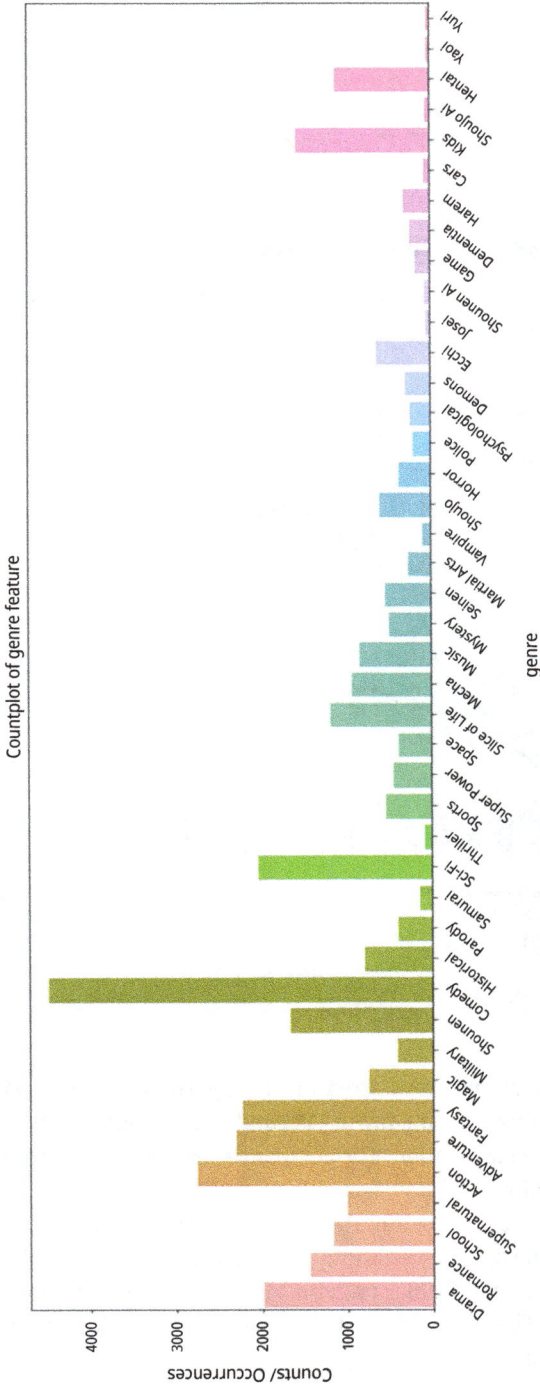

Figure 9.2: Exploratory Data Analysis on Anime Data (Vinayak Nayak, 2020).
Genre count – Source: https://towardsdatascience.com/exploratory-data-analysis-on-anime-data-468cc15e13b8 Data (not the latest) – *Source:* https://www.kaggle.com/CooperUnion/anime-recommendations-database?select=anime.csv

(a)

(b)

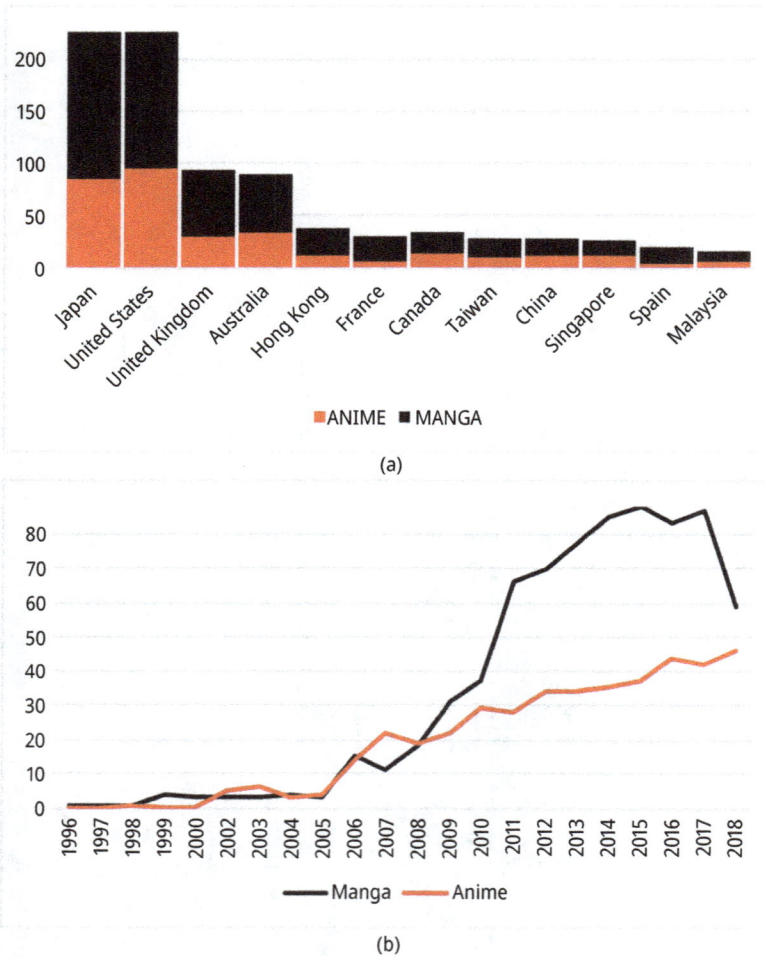

Figure 9.3: Literature mention of Anime and Manga.
Source: M. Hernández-Pérez (2019)

A Silent Voice (2016), etc. Kyoto Animation was started in 1981 by Yoko and Hideaki Hatta, a married couple; it became a limited company in 1985 and a corporation in 1999. Yoko Hatta is the vice president of the corporation. The company's logo originates from the *kanji kyō* (京), the first character of Kyoto.

Kyoto Animation since 2009 has been hosting the Kyoto Animation Awards in three categories: original novels, manga, and scenarios. Some of the winning submissions are published under the KA Esuma Bunko imprint and may be adapted into anime in the future. In 2014 *Violet Evergarden* was the first and only work to have won a grand prize in all three categories.

Kyoto Animation is recognized for its high-quality production values and "sensitivity" to the work and quandaries of ordinary life. Unlike other animation studios, the company's employees are salaried rather than freelancers, and they receive on-the-job training. Employees have been more encouraged to focus on frame quality rather than production limits because of these techniques. Women in Animation awarded the company the Diversity Award in 2020 for its efforts in developing a gender-balanced workforce and encouraging women to enter the profession, and the company has won recognition for its friendly treatment of its employees.

Quality

KyoAni's ability to evoke images that are patently artificial but feel consummately real is memorably demonstrated in all its productions by using real-life locations as the basis for its settings, to pay homage to their distinctive features with naturalistic punctiliousness, and immerse them in a magical atmosphere that places them well beyond simple photojournalism. This effect is accomplished by treating the materials gleaned through fieldwork as sources of inspiration, and as springboards to autonomous artistic expression and creative experiment, not as fixed templates to be robotically reproduced.

They also embrace cultural polyphony in an inimitable fashion by discreetly heeding back to tradition through several of their recurrent topoi (rhetoric argument), yet also striking very contemporary notes or even venturing into futuristically speculative scenarios. The material interplay of diverse reality levels finds a correlative in a philosophical perspective that has consistently pervaded Japanese mythology, literature, and popular culture: the conception of the boundaries supposedly separating reality from fantasy and facts from dreams as tenuous, unpredictable, and ultimately unreliable. In artistic terms, this stance has typically resulted in a distinctive integration of serenity and turbulence, harmony and strife, playfulness, and belligerence as interpenetrating processes rather than mutually incompatible states.

Arson Attack

Kyoto Animation has been slowly making a comeback since approximately 36 employees were killed in a catastrophic arson attack in July 2019. The attack resulted in causalities of over 40% of the studio's employees, forcing the firm to temporarily halt its training program and new hires. However, in autumn last year, the studio resumed operations while continuing to produce new films. Despite the devastating attack, the studio continued to work on a new anime feature, *Violet Evergarden: The Movie*, which was supposed to be released in April but has since been postponed due to the

COVID-19 outbreak. The film is described as "a work developed by our employees with tremendous enthusiasm" on Kyoto Animation's official website.

Overall Impact of Anime

KyoAni is known for having excellent visual and animation quality in all its works. When so many other studios, especially for dedicated idol shows, will use CGI 3D animation to animate the dance sequences, KyoAni does things like hand animating a throw-away idol dance scene. *Violet Evergarden* and *Miss Kobayashi's Dragon Maid* are two of KyoAni's most visually stunning works. *Violet Evergarden* succeeds at being highly realistic, and it was a great showcase for KyoAni's animation method and engine, which they were eager to show off. Switching gears to *Dragon Maid,* the show has a much simpler style than *Violet Evergarden,* with a more "watercolor" like style. Despite its simplicity, the animation isn't thoughtless or low quality.

Violet Evergarden is visually a spectacular show, and it beautifully explores the story of a young girl returning from war, attempting to reintegrate into society, focusing on helping others, not giving up, values and hardships of trying to live a normal life, and a lot more important experiences. So far the anime has received outstanding reviews for its impact on people and the industry, not to mention the quality and detailing of the anime.

Another great example, *Kobayashi Dragon Maid,* talks about a normal salaried working woman who comes across a dragon and how they start living together. This anime has a detailed animation style conveying heartwarming messages about life, friends, and trust.

Business and Working

KyoAni's business models and main sources of revenues consist of blu-rays/DVDs, publications, animation books, figurines, posters, etc. According to the financial reports of KyoAni, they have shown a revenue of 2.3 billion yen ($19 million) and a net profit of 165,301,000 yen ($1.3 million) for the year ending March 2019. The arson attack was one of the important reasons for the growth of the studio.

Most anime studios are just contractors on the project, and only get paid to cover the cost of production, hence, earning a small profit. Since they aren't invested in the production committee, they earn the same whether a show sells 500 copies or 50,000. Merchandise is a good way to support anime, but that money gets split between the main investors (record companies, model kit and figurine companies, etc.) and the original creator. However, KyoAni and a few of the most successful studios invest in their own shows and make more money if it does well. This is a strategy that has proved to be very beneficial for KyoAni and has helped them achieve the success they have today.

The attack didn't reduce their willpower and determination. Looking at their confidence and hard work, a lot of funds were raised for the studio to help them recover their losses. After everything, they managed to release two of the top grossing animes, *Violet Evergarden* and Kobayashi's *Dragon Maid*. This also increased their local acceptance and global reputation. Since anime and anime-related products demand started increasing globally, this gave them yet another opportunity to pull through and deliver amazing results for their fans all over the world.

Conclusion

Most of the studios follow a milker strategy, that is, they try to get a chunk off the popular idea/ product in the market. Kyoto Animation, however, are movers. They employ new techniques and always look into innovative ideas, adapting and improving the source material to come up with new ground-breaking and market capturing ideas, not to mention animation that is years ahead of its time. The studio has a great reputation both locally and globally. They are financially stable and independent and have a team of employees that are adaptable and are always looking for more talented people.

Anime is, in the end, a niche product in Japan that is growing increasingly competitive, and as a result, is heavily reliant on outside sales. Anime studios regularly construct and reference from what might be described as a database to support that success. It's a database of elements that can be used to identify content as being particularly anime. Anime characteristics can include everything from animation style to character traits to genres and cliches. The important thing is to be able to deliver what the fans need and the quality, which Kyoto Animation has given a very promising result to.

References

Websites

https://www.looper.com/177480/the-best-anime-of-the-past-decade/
https://socrogueScholars.wordpress.com/2016/09/24/anime-globalization-is-vast-and-infinite/
https://www.liveabout.com/brief-history-of-anime-144979
https://books.google.co.in/books?hl=en&lr=&id=wWmZRGfqIBcC&oi=fnd&pg=PP1&dq=Kyoto+Animatio
    n&ots=YKg4NcXgNN&sig=wlgAkj2XMqZbTcZevrMdlLkGqbQ&redir_esc=y#v=onepage&q&f=false
https://towardsdatascience.com/exploratory-data-analysis-on-anime-data-468cc15e13b8
https://www.grandviewresearch.com/press-release/global-anime-market

https://cultureofgaming.com/kyoto-animations-impact-on-anime/; https://www.slideshare.net/Adriel
Leung/kyoto-animation-company-preso
https://www.futuremarketinsights.com/reports/anime-market#:~:text=Anime%20Market%20Outlook%20
(2022%E2%80%932032,according%20to%20the%20FMI%20assessment. (Accessed on
11 November 2022).

Articles and Books

Cooper, L. M. (2010). Right Stuf Anime. https://www.rightstufanime.com/anime-resources-global-history-
of-anime
D.B. (2017). One angry gamer. https://www.oneangrygamer.net/2017/06/tekken-7-story-mode-
walkthrough-and-ending-explained/31986/
Grand View Research (2021). Anime Market Size Worth $48.03 Billion by 2028. https://www.grandviewre
search.com/press-release/global-anime-market
Dani Cavallaro (2012). Kyoto Animation: A Critical Study and Filmography. https://books.google.co.in/
books?hl=en&id=wWmZRGfqIBcC&oi=fnd&pg=PP1&dq=Kyoto+Animation&ots=YKg4NcXgNN&sig=
wlgAkj2XMqZbTcZevrMdILkGqbQ&redir_esc=y#v=onepage&q&f=false
Hernández-Pérez, M. (2019). Looking into the "Anime Global Popular" and the "Manga Media": Reflections
on the Scholarship of a Transnational and Transmedia Industry. *Arts*, *8*(2), 57. https://doi.org/
10.3390/arts8020057
Honey's Anime (2018). Violet Evergarden Review – "I want to know. I love you." https://honeysanime.com/
violet-evergarden-review-i-want-to-know-i-love-you/
Juliet Kah (2019). The Best Anime of the Past Decade. https://www.looper.com/177480/the-best-anime-of-
the-past-decade/
Krishnan, C., Gupta, A., Gupta, A., Singh, G. (2022). Impact of Artificial Intelligence-Based Chatbots on
Customer Engagement and Business Growth. In: Hong, TP., Serrano-Estrada, L., Saxena, A., Biswas,
A. (eds) *Deep Learning for Social Media Data Analytics. Studies in Big Data*, vol 113. Springer, Cham.
https://doi.org/10.1007/978-3-031-10869-3_11
Kyoto Animation's Impact on Anime: Culture of Gaming, https://cultureofgaming.com/kyoto-animations-
impact-on-anime/
Lauren Orsini (2019). After Arson Attack, Fans Raise Over $5 Million For Kyoto Animation. https://www.for
bes.com/sites/laurenorsini/2019/07/26/after-arson-attack-fans-raise-over-5-million-for-kyoto-
animation/?sh=427a222e7cb2
Matthew Chase (2016). Anime: Globalization is Vast and Infinite. Anime: Globalization is Vast and Infinite –
SocRogueScholars (wordpress.com)
Serdar Yegulalp (2019). Brief History of Anime. https://www.liveabout.com/brief-history-of-anime-144979
Spirited Away, directed by Hayao Miyazaki. https://irevise.com/ie/exams/junior-cert/english/notes/spir
ited-away-directed-by-hayao-miyazaki
TPC Desk (2021). Why Should You Watch "Jujutsu Kaisen" If Anime Interests. https://www.thepolicychro
nicle.co.in/why-should-you-watch-jujutsu-kaisen-if-anime-interests-you/.
Ulrich Heinze (2012). Time travel topoi in Japanese manga, Japan Forum, 24:2, 163–184, DOI: 10.1080/
09555803.2012.671844
Vinayak Nayak (2020). Exploratory Data Analysis on Anime Data.https://towardsdatascience.com/explor
atory-data-analysis-on-anime-data-468cc15e13b8

Ron Sheffield
Chapter 10
Crossing all Borders – The Future of IoT

Yesterday – Our Desire to Connect

Social science research seeks to understand how the world around us influences our very existence. I might suggest that the earliest humans sought more than just food and shelter. They likely sought, much like today, to understand the meaning of life and maybe to connect with peers a little more each day. This search for connectivity, while likely always tiring, has always circled around basic forms of human communication. As people sought the wisdom of others through discussion or written communications, many have also likely sought to grasp increasing levels of control over their environment. These forms of control have most readily evolved into formalized religion, governments, and schools. Does everyone that lives near us really need to learn the exact same information to be considered a citizen? While ominous in tone, the intent was likely not always malicious.

As we sought to trade services and products with each other, we were also challenged with the concept of "more versus less" and how that culturally driven social measurement felt internally when we looked in the mirror. Psychologically and practically, I don't believe we've evolved very much from the first moment that we started trading with each other. However, I do believe we have added business models and theories to hide our contempt or pleasure for an unruly internal emotion called greed. Have we always sought to control? Do we seek control because we are owed something more than we have? Do we really need more? Maybe or maybe not. For one moment, if we attempt to see the world through the eyes of the Indigenous people of North America, we might consider a unique form of understanding. After all, as stewards of this land for over 15,000 years, Indigenous peoples might just know how to govern, learn, and foster effective forms of communications.

Today – We Believe in the Future of Technology

Many people that work within the technology discipline today see themselves, largely, as "original thinkers" of modern computer technology. While this could not be further from the truth, the application of newer technology does allow us to see, hear, and even record an experience with relative ease. We then use this recording to playback a moment of time and then assign judgement to the actions witnessed. This new form of image capture allows us to be seduced into believing that we "know" more than yesterday. The movement and growth of technology does not remain stationary. A

https://doi.org/10.1515/9783110734133-010

consideration of this continuous change is reflected with the latest updates within the manufacturing industry. Industry 5.0 has arrived and this branded movement of human interaction with machinery provides an interesting glimpse into our technological future.

Industry 5.0

According to Carayannis et al. (2020), "Industry 5.0 is considered to be the answer to the question of a renewed human centered/human centric industrial paradigm, starting from the (structural, organizational, managerial, knowledge-based, philosophical, and cultural) reorganization of the production processes of industry" (p. 1892). By examining the future use and application of global fusion energy, Carayannis et al. draw upon the concept of "growth" as being a good thing. This is an assumption that many people will challenge as science and technology bully their way into our daily lives. We can assume that economics and capitalism provide the lubricant necessary to build new forms of energy that are most-often cloaked in the dressage of peace, harmony, and love for humankind. But wait . . . there's more! If we assume that the progression of the Internet of Things (IoT) is "good," when does it become too good? Or too much? Or just ill-placed?

Without a prescribed limitation to most things, humankind is likely to repeat itself. If left unchecked, people will often consume all the nutrients from a forest and, as we've been known to do, deplete the planet's resources with the mantra of "this is right because of the good of many." We kill animals and people in the name of "progress" just as many families gather each week to pray for health and prosperity on Sunday morning. Does my ability to see my dog on a remote camera mean I'm prosperous? Does my ever-expanding property fence-line mean I'm prosperous? I watched the news recently where a man was able to see his grandfather on his smartphone camera just before he died of COVID-19. Does this mean he's prosperous? Let's examine a few perspectives on using IoT to monitor human performance and mental workloads.

Monitoring

Internationally, the foundational ideas surrounding IoT could largely be reduced to some basic perspectives: speed of data, behaviors and data output, money, and human interaction with a given task. Pütz et al. (2022) surveyed 702 managers within three European countries (United Kingdom, Spain, and Germany) regarding their expectations and concerns on human workload monitoring. In summary, human workload monitoring is as it reads: monitoring human workload through IoT devices. Not surprisingly, according to Putz et al., "one of the main findings of this study is the major role of privacy concerns, as it was the most prevalent concern in quantitative ratings, by far the most frequent concern in open responses and showed the strongest association with system support" (p. 102). Translation: employees and their managers do not trust their employers to use IoT for the good of humanity. Time and experience have taught us that greed often masks itself in the sparkle of proposed "love and care." One significant difference between today and yesterday, regarding our work environment, is the use of near-instant global communications. The manager and employee can gain basic understanding of most workplace technologies rather quickly these days.

So, are we prepared to go backwards? Do we believe that the international marketplace will use IoT to monitor employee health for the benefit of the employee? Sure, they will . . . and just like the advent of "marketing," which began its roots focused on gaining greater understanding of human behavior, the use of marketing today is no longer cloaked in secrecy. We use marketing to make money and just in case the reader might be thinking, "not always!," please reflect on a single instance where money or power weren't readily visible just below the surface with any marketing campaign.

Data

According to Ahmed and Mohamed,

> data is at the heart of the digital age or, as some put it, "the new oil," "the next natural resource" and the "currency of the 21st century" that everything depends on to function and operate. The IoT, which aims to connect things to the Internet and interconnect them with each other, could have a huge impact on data generation and dissemination as there will be data streams from countless sources. The centrality of data and its countless value in today's world do not, however, end contention and controversial views about its nature. (2020, p. 81)

However, does data really constitute a lubricant worthy of the moniker, "next natural resource"? Maybe not. Data, as it is used today, and very likely tomorrow, is oftentimes a moment of documented human behavior. While we do indeed seek to learn from captured human moments, the power of this experience is more likely the capture of a crystalized ill-understood and uncontextualized experience. Data is nothing without analysis and for our modern economically driven society, analysis is nothing without monetization. Yes, I realize that this is a harsh statement. However, there are very few examples of mass data capturing where money wasn't a key driver of either the capturing or analysis of the data under scrutiny.

Data capture and analysis is not necessarily the scariest part of the IoT future. However, many of the facets surrounding data capture will wreak havoc on platform designers as IoT matures. Ahmed and Mohamed (2020) deem this the "propertization of data" (p. 84). Legal challenges will abound as IoT captures our daily lives in minute segments.

Just as many businesses do today, data will be sought to capitalize on captured human behaviors. The idea of legal challenges with data usage is not new at this point. The future of IoT is likely to introduce a form of "intellectual social data property." This type of intelligence-driven property will be neither owned nor monetized for everyone. Instead, this form of data, driven and produced through the discreet data collection methods cloaked as "IoT," will provide legal scholars and technology architects a new vision for data ownership. So, who will own this information? While this is unknown, the social scientist would posit that all data started as freely shared human behavior points and those experiences, while they hold enormous value, should never be limited to the confines of monetization. What happens when we freely grant access to others surrounding our inner-most thoughts that have been translated onto an electronic media? When does data capturing become invasive if we buy the device and ask it what the weather is today? We should fully expect that the money paid for that hardware translates into an exponentially higher revenue for the one listening on the other end.

Social Networks

At some point during our social media engagements, many of us have witnessed the online dancing cat, the ill clothed "influencer," an angrily cloaked meme, or possibly a proudly posed recent graduate. On January 6th, 2021, social media provided the targeted delivery of hate-laced messaging which served to fuel a few of the most unsettled citizens across America. On this date, people from across the United States illustrated a public act of domestic terrorism by entering the United States Capitol during a session of Congress. Was social media partially accountable for this horrendous act? Maybe. This logic is a slippery slope to follow and if we keep this momentum moving, we might soon assume that IoT may become somewhat responsible for harm to our fellow citizens. With this in mind, Baltoi (2020) posits that "social media can be defined as a set of communication channels through which users create communities and share information, ideas, personal messages and other content (photos, videos, music, etc.)" (p. 63). Baltoi goes on to suggest that IoT "integration will pave the way for new social monitoring tools to harness the information transmitted by millions of interconnected smart objects. Among the various currently available objects, we have WiFi Routers, WiFi or NFC tags, motion sensors, gesture recognition sensors, etc." (2020, p. 69). Interestingly, there is little downside written about IoT or Social Networks within the academic research. I surmise that Baltoi's words serve to explain the lack of this critical analysis in this way, "currently, large companies are trying to integrate more and more the use of IoT to monitor user activities and habits" (p. 69). Just for a moment, ask yourself the question, "Why do large companies, or any company, wish to integrate this technology to observe human behavior?"

The wisest choice that any governing entity may undertake is to allow its partici-pants the perception of free will and intellectual freedom. By granting the idea of free thought to many, a few will craft new and innovative forms of human connectivity that could have otherwise taken a lifetime to create. Our culture makes many assump-tions about "right and wrong," "good and bad," and "smart or not." Often, we base those fundamental concepts within the boundaries of money and then assume them to be "good." As brilliant ideas emerge, if people continue to assume that wealth equals good and poor equals bad, we remain highly susceptible to manipulation. Human imagination has a long history of fruitful production, and a list of our innova-tions is far too large to capture. However, a few that come to mind: electricity, the control of water, cars, guns, telephones, internet, social networks, and so on. There is little doubt that our management of these wonderful inventions has delivered amaz-ing results for the good of humankind. In contrast, we can easily see the harm that is produced by monetizing the most basic forms of human connectivity.

Future – Full Circle? Back to Smoke Signals?

Assume that human beings are at some point able to 'control' all of the inanimate ob-jects around them with the click of a button, wave of the hand, flicker of the eye, or by thought. Where do we move from that point? Without question, humans will re-turn to the original intent of sender-receiver communications which is to assure safe passage of a critical message. One such example of a critical message considers the safety of those within a confined space.

Intimate partner violence (IPV) continues to plague societies across the globe in 2022 and, in part, through the application of IoT, people may find some relief to help combat this treatment. According to Rodriguez, "Variables such as exercise, move-ment, heart rate temperature, perspiration, location, velocity and acceleration in mo-tion can be taken into account in order to check abnormal variations caused by physical violence" (2020, p. 3).

The smartphone, while an early form of the IoT movement, has proven to be a weapon like none other in modern society. Verbal stories that were previously shared by those without powerful economic or societal positions were often largely consid-ered inaccurate or even pure falsehoods. The advent of the smartphone, accompanied with the ease of use of its video functionality, has provided visual evidence where few words were required to explain.

The reader may be considering, "why does this chapter focus on the harms that technologies have illuminated and not all of the positives?" That's a great question and is worthy of heart-felt consideration. Technology may be a means by which we make money, live a questionably more "efficient" life, or enable our coffee maker be-fore stumbling out of bed to start the day. However, IoT, along with all technologies, should be harnessed to provide real power to those unable to have a voice. All humans start this world as part of a tribe of people and from this basic origination point, people seek to communicate their loves, passions, and fears with others. Unfortunately, it's the sharing of "fear" where some often seek to intervene and stop the transfer of data. Few of our daily lives are lacking media stories of hope, triumphant glimpses of heroism, or even smiling birthday announcements. However, very rarely do we see or hear of other's pains and struggles often experienced behind closed doors. Good grief, we can't even take a single picture of ourselves without scrolling for minutes to hours for "just the right angle" to post on a simple form of social media.

The evolution of technology has a purpose, and that purpose should always be to help humankind without an agenda of suppression or repression. IoT will continue to gain speed and perpetually ooze its way into the intimate moments of our day. We, as the authors and creators of these technologies need only to heed the words of my mom before she died some years ago. While crafting my doctoral research, I asked my mom about questioning the elders of our tribe. Sheila Palone Sheffield, a full-blood Quechan Native American/Indigenous woman, raised on our reservation in Winterhaven, California responded, "Be careful what you ask and be prepared to hear nothing."

References

Ahmed, S. M. S., & Mohamed, D. (2020). Data in the Internet of Things Era: The Propertization of Data in Light of Contemporary Business Practices. *International Journal of Business & Society, 21*, 81–94.

BĂLȚOI, I.-C.-M. (2020). Integration of Emerging Technologies into Social Networks. *Informatica Economica, 24*(1), 61–74. https://doi.org/10.24818/issn14531305/24.1.2020.06

Carayannis, E.G., Draper, J., & Bhaneja, B. Towards Fusion Energy in the Industry 5.0 and Society 5.0 Context: Call for a Global Commission for Urgent Action on Fusion Energy. *Journal of Knowledge Economy* (2020). https://doi-org.echo.louisville.edu/10.1007/s13132-020-00695-5

Oztemel, E., & Gursev, S. (2020). Literature Review of Industry 4.0 and Related Technologies. *Journal of Intelligent Manufacturing, 31*(1), 127–182. https://doi.org/10.1007/s10845-018-1433-8

Pütz, S., Rick, V., Mertens, A., & Nitsch, V. (2022). Using iot devices for sensor-based monitoring of employees' mental workload: investigating managers' expectations and concerns. *Applied Ergonomics, 102*, 103739–103739. https://doi.org/10.1016/j.apergo.2022.103739

Rodríguez-Rodríguez, I., Rodríguez, J.-V., Elizondo-Moreno, A., Heras-González, P., & Gentili, M. (2020). Towards a Holistic ICT Platform for Protecting Intimate Partner Violence Survivors Based on the IoT Paradigm. *Symmetry* (20738994), *12*(1), 37. https://doi.org/10.3390/sym12010037

List of Figures

https://doi.org/10.1515/9783110734133-011

List of Tables

https://doi.org/10.1515/9783110734133-012

List of Contributors

Aldo Alvarez-Risco is an associate professor at the Universidad de Lima. He has a master's degree in pharmacology and PhD in pharmacy and biochemistry at Universidad Nacional Mayor de San Marcos.

Soma Arora is a professor at Manav Rachna International Institute of Research and Studies (MRIIRS) in the faculty of management studies. She specializes in marketing/international business and analytics, at post-graduate levels in internationally recognized, AACSB and DEAC accredited institutions.

Shyla Del-Aguila-Arcentales has a master's degree in pharmaceuticals from Universidad Nacional Mayor de San Marcos and is a professor at Escuela Nacional de Marina Mercante "Almirante Miguel Grau" (ENAMM).

Aditya Kumar Gupta is an associate professor at Amity University, Noida, India. He is a certified case trainer from Harvard Business School and IIM-Ahmedabad marketing research trainer from IIM-Lucknow. He has 20 years of experience teaching marketing and international business to students of undergraduate, postgraduate, and research scholars. He is an editor and reviewer of a number of reputable journals and presented research papers at various national and international conferences. He has conducted training and workshops in the area of digital marketing, rural marketing, branding, consumer behavior, and student engagement.

Virginia Hernández is assistant professor at University Carlos III of Madrid (Spain). Her research interests include entrepreneurship, digitalization, and internationalization, especially on SMEs. She has published in top journals such as *Long Range Planning, Journal of World Business,* and *Global Strategy Journal,* among others.

Chaitanya Kohli is an MBA from IMT Ghaziabad. He is working with M-INSURE, an Insuretech, Health Tech Company, as a founding team member. He handles product development, strategy, and alliances at M-INSURE.

Letitia Larry is an executive-level development operations (DevOps) information technology consultant with more than 20 years of experience, specializing in epic solutions, systems, services, and human capital transformations across federal agencies and commercial enterprises. Dr. Larry earned an EdD in human and organizational learning from George Washington University and holds an MS in computer information systems and a BS in applied mathematics. Dr. Larry is also a certified project management professional (PMP) and continues to expand her experience and expertise as a scholar and practitioner.

Nathalie de Marcellis-Warin is a full professor at Polytechnique Montreal, Department of Mathematics and Industrial Engineering, president and chief executive officer at CIRANO, and co-PI of the Observatory on the Societal Impacts of AI and Digital Technologies (OBVIA).

Alka Maurya is a professor with Amity International Business School, Amity University, India. She is a computer science graduate and has her master's degree and PhD in international business. She has over 26 years of experience in teaching, research, and consulting. She has worked with various trade promotion organizations before going into academics. She is invited as speaker/resource person for various international/national conferences and seminars in the area of international business. She has published several books and research papers/case studies in her area of specialization. Teaching is her passion, and she is engaged in shaping young minds to accept the challenges in this dynamic and competitive environment.

https://doi.org/10.1515/9783110734133-013

J. Mark Munoz holds an MBA and PhD in management. He is a tenured full professor of management at Millikin University, and a former visiting fellow at the Kennedy School of Government at Harvard University. He received several awards, including four best research paper awards, two international book awards, a literary award, the ACBSP Teaching Excellence Award (one of 10 in the world), Distinguished Business Dean Award and the Global Academic Excellence Award among others. Aside from top-tier journal publications, he has authored/edited/co-edited more than 20 books such as *Global Business Intelligence, The Handbook of Artificial Intelligence and Robotic Process Automation, The Economics of Cryptocurrencies,* and *The AI Leader.* He serves on corporate and editorial boards, and assists companies and countries in international marketing, finance, and business development.

Agnieszka Olter has an MSc in international economic relations from the Cracow University of Economics and is currently pursuing doctoral studies in political sciences and public administration at the University of Warsaw. She is a lecturer in the double degree program at the University of London.

RJ Podeschi is dean of the Tabor School of Business and associate professor of information systems at Millikin University in Decatur, Illinois. He has over a decade of IT experience and leadership, in addition to launching a local IT consulting firm. His primary research and teaching interests include information systems pedagogy, business intelligence and analytics, and cybersecurity; specifically, how best to build the necessary skills for a 21st-century workforce.

Antonio Revilla is associate professor at Management University Carlos III of Madrid (Spain). His research interests include R&D management strategies, the globalization of the innovation value chain, and innovation in family businesses. He has published his research in journals such as *Family Business Review, Technovation,* and *British Journal of Management,* among others.

Alicia Rodríguez is associate professor at Carlos III University of Madrid. Her research interests include digital entrepreneurship, internationalization, and innovation, with a special focus on SMEs. Her research appears in top journals such as *Journal of International Business Studies, Strategic Management Journal,* and *Long Range Planning,* among others.

Guido Rojer Jr. is a specialist in island studies, focusing on private sector organizations (Island Based Firms). He has extensive experience as an executive director as well as in various supervision roles, and lectures in business at the University of Curaçao Business School. He is a PhD candidate in economics and business at the UNED Madrid, holds an MSc in public policy from Maastricht University, and a BSc in international business from the University of Curaçao.

Dr. Ron Sheffield, EdD, PMP, CSM, SAFe, RODC, SSBB, CCP is a member of the Quechan Indian Tribe of Yuma Arizona and Winterhaven California. He is currently an Executive in Residence, Clinical Assistant Professor, and Program Director of the Master of Science Degree Program in Human Resources and Organization Development (HR/OD) at The University of Louisville. Dr. Sheffield is also Founder and President of OrgScience, Inc, a United States based Professional Services Consultancy focused on enterprise technology and organization health.

Hugo Warin is a software engineer student at Polytechnique Montreal (Canada).

Thierry Warin is a full professor of data science at HEC Montreal (Canada) and director of the Open Data Lab at CIRANO (Montreal, Canada).

About the Editors

Alka Maurya is a professor at Amity International Business School, Amity University, India. She is a Computer Science graduate and has a Masters and Ph.D. in International Business. She has over 26 years of experience in teaching, research and consulting and has received several national and international awards for her work in research and teaching.

Before joining academics she worked with National Centre for Trade Information, which is a UN designated Trade Point in India, and Plastics Export Promotion Council, an autonomous body under the Ministry of Commerce. At both these places she was associated with various initiatives related to promoting exports from India.

Dr. Maurya has been invited as keynote speaker/resource person for various international/national conferences and seminars in the area of International Business. She has published several books and research papers/case studies in her area of specialization. Teaching is her passion, and she is shaping young minds to take up the challenges of today's dynamic and competitive environment.

J. Mark Munoz is an MBA graduate and PhD in Management. He is a tenured Full Professor of Management at Millikin University, and a former Visiting Fellow at the Kennedy School of Government at Harvard University. He served as Advisor to the AI Initiative at Harvard University (The Future Society). At Millikin, he received several awards such as the Teaching Excellence Award, Research and Artistic Achievement Award and the Teaching Excellence and Campus Leadership Award. Internationally, he has been recognized with four Best Research Paper Awards, two international book awards, a literary award, the ACBSP Teaching Excellence Award (one of 10 in the world), Distinguished Business Dean Award and the Global Academic Excellence Award, among others. Aside from top-tier journal publications, he has authored/edited more than 25 books such as: *Handbook on the Geopolitics of Business*, *Advances in Geoeconomics*, *Global Business Intelligence*, *The Handbook of Artificial Intelligence and Robotic Process Automation*, *The Economics of Cryptocurrencies* and *The AI Leader*. He is also the Chairman/CEO of the international management consulting firm, Munoz and Associates International. He serves in corporate and editorial boards, and assists companies and countries in international marketing, finance and business development.

Loveleen Gaur is the Professor and Program Director (Artificial Intelligence and Business Intelligence and Data Analytics) at Amity International Business School, Amity University, Noida, India. She is an established author and researcher and has filed five patents and two copyrights in AI-IoT. She is actively involved in various reputed projects of Government of India and abroad and has contributed significantly to enhancing scientific understanding by participating in over three hundred scientific conferences, symposia, and seminars, and by chairing technical sessions and delivering plenary and invited talks. Prof. Gaur specializes in the fields of Artificial Intelligence, Internet of Things, Data Analytics, Data Mining and Business Intelligence. She has pursued research in truly inter-disciplinary areas and authored and co-authored books with renowned international and national publishers like Elsevier, Springer, and Taylor & Francis. She has been an invited Guest Editor for Springer NASA journals and Emerald Q1 journals and has published many research papers in SCI and Q1 journals. She is a senior IEEE member and series editor with CRC and Wiley.

https://doi.org/10.1515/9783110734133-014

Prof. Gaur has been honored with prestigious national and international awards like "Senior Women Educator & Scholar Award" by National Foundation for Entrepreneurship Development on Women's Day, "Sri Ram Award" by Delhi Management Association (DMA) and "Distinguished Research Award" by Allied Academies.

Gurinder Singh, PhD, is Group Vice Chancellor of Amity Universities, Uttar Pradesh, India and Director General of Amity International Business School. Professor Singh has extensive experience of more than 21 years in institutional building, teaching, consultancy, research, and industry. Dr. Singh is a renowned scholar and academician in international business, he holds a prestigious doctorate in the area along with a postgraduate degree from the Indian Institute of Foreign Trade, where he illustriously topped with seven merits. He holds the distinction of being the youngest Founder Pro-Vice-Chancellor of Amity University for two terms and the Founder Director General of Amity International Business School and the Founder CEO of the Association of International Business Schools, London. He has been instrumental in establishing various Amity campuses abroad. He has received more than 25 international and national awards and has graced a host of talk shows on various TV channels. He is a mesmerizing orator and has the rare ability of touching the human soul.

Index

https://doi.org/10.1515/9783110734133-015

www.ingramcontent.com/pod-product-compliance
Lightning Source LLC
Chambersburg PA
CBHW081520190326
41458CB00015B/5416